Felt, Fabric, and Fiber
JEWELRY

FELT, FABRIC, AND FIBER JEWELRY

20 Beautiful Projects to Bead, Stitch, Knot, and Braid

Sherri Haab

Watson-Guptill Publications

New York

Executive Editor: Joy Acquilino

Editor: Martha Moran

Production Manager: Alyn Evans

Book Designer: Jooyoung Lee

Photographs: Dan and Sherri Haab, Zachary Williams

Illustrations: Sherri Haab and Sherry Polley

Text, projects, designs, illustrations, and technical how-to photographs
© 2008 by Dan and Sherri Haab, except as otherwise noted

Jewelry and still life photographs © 2008 by Zachary Williams

Cover photography ©2008 by Zachary Williams

Crochet illustrations ©2005 by Watson-Guptill Publications

First published in 2008 by Watson-Guptill Publications

Nielsen Business Media,

a division of The Nielsen Company

770 Broadway

New York, New York 10003

www.watsonguptill.com

Library of Congress Cataloging-in-Publication Number: 2007941629

ISBN-13: 978-0-8230-9909-2

ISBN-10: 0-8230-9909-1

All rights reserved. No part of this publication may be reproduced or used in any form or by any means—
graphic, electronic, or mechanical, including photocopying, recording, taping, or information storage and
retrieval systems—without written permission of the publisher.

Watson-Guptill Publications books are available at special discounts when purchased in bulk for premiums and
sales promotions, as well as for fund-raising or educational use. Special editions or book excerpts can be created
to specification. For details, please contact the Special Sales Director at the address above.

Manufactured in China

First printing, 2008

1 2 3 4 5 6 7 8 9 / 16 15 14 13 12 11 10 09 08

Dedication

Dedicated to my Mom, Shirley, who taught me how to sew and
encouraged creativity when I was young.

Acknowledgments

To Dan, for your support and help with photos.

To Michelle, Mary, Rachel, and Lisa for contributing fabulous projects.

To my daughter, Michelle, for her creative ideas.

To Camille for hand modelling.

Many thanks to the manufacturers who supplied materials for the book.

My gratitude to the staff at Watson-Guptill for their dedication and support of this book.

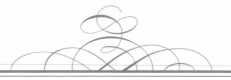

Contents

part 2 : projects

introduction

TRADITIONALLY one might first think of metal, stone, or glass in reference to jewelry making, but un-conventional materials such as fabric, felt, and fibers hold a strong presence in the world of jewelry making. Since ancient times, objects worn for adornment were fashioned not only from metal or stone, but from softer materials including fibers, feathers, leather, braided cord, even hair. Throughout history, artisans used materials that were easily accessible to them, combining a variety of materials (precious and non-precious) to create jewelry.

To me there is something refreshing about an artist who dares to "color outside the lines" when it comes to jewelry making. When someone creates a piece of jewelry out of unexpected materials that are not considered to be precious at all, it prompts one to rethink the perception of those materials. Ordinary, inexpensive, or unconventional items are assigned a new perceived value because the artist found significance in the materials and thoughtfully crafted them into a wearable piece of art. Materials such as fabric scraps, ribbon, vintage cord, and colorful pieces of felt evoke nostalgic memories for some, and simply a pleasant tactile experience for others.

The projects in this book were all created using traditional fiber and needlework techniques. New products, jewelry findings, and craft materials have been combined with these techniques to create jewelry with a fresh modern twist. You may find that the creation process is as much fun as the end result, as repetitive needlecrafts like crocheting, stitching, or knotting are very relaxing. Most of these projects are small and portable making them perfect to take along for travel or for something to do while sitting in a waiting room. Best of all, the projects are quick to make. If you love to sew but don't have the time or feel inclined to make clothing, you can make a hand-stitched piece of jewelry that will give you equal satisfaction. You might find a new needlecraft you haven't thought to try before but now have the opportunity to sample the craft on a small project. Enjoy stitching, braiding, and knotting your way through the projects in this book!

THE BASICS

Materials

YOU MAY ALREADY have the materials needed for the projects in this book. Many of my designs were inspired by digging through my sewing box or sorting through the random craft supplies I had on hand. Most of the materials are generic in nature and can easily be substituted with a similar item you may have in your stash.

○ sources for materials ○

The materials and supplies needed for the projects in this book consist of sewing, craft, and home office supplies. Use your own favorite fabric scraps, vintage beads, or personal collectibles. Most of the tools and supplies for the projects follow the same logic—you can easily substitute a different sized sewing or crochet needle, use a similar tool, or use a compatible adhesive depending on your preference or what is easily accessible.

I try to use recycled or otherwise discarded materials whenever possible as these can be worked into a finished design. Or they can be used as tools in the construction process. For example, the cardboard from cereal boxes is perfect for cutting into templates for patterns.

Since materials, yarn styles, and craft supplies might be discontinued or hard to source, take comfort in the fact that the supplies for these projects are not so specific that you cannot create them if a particular item cannot be found. The fun part of making a craft is the creativity you put into the piece. Choosing your own personal components gives you the freedom to use the colors, textures, and design elements that speak to you, allowing you to create a OOAK (one of a kind) works of art.

○ felt, fabric, and fiber ○

I usually think of fabric as being divided into two categories: natural and synthetic. Natural fabrics such as cotton, silk, and wool felt bring to mind soft, earthy accessories with a casual elegance—think of traditional cotton quilts, vintage handkerchiefs, and hand-spun, dyed wool. Jewelry made with fabric will compliment a fashionable outfit by extending its texture and color. Old clothing or fabric scraps provide a vast resource for jewelry making since even the smallest piece can be utilized in the design. Natural fibers can be given an aged appearance by soaking them in coffee or tea.

Synthetic fabrics such as nylon, polyester, or synthetic/natural blends give you options for manipulating the fibers to accommodate a design. Synthetic

fibers melt with heat, allowing you to seal the edges to prevent fraying. Nylon cord ends that are finished with heat instead of glue give you a more professional result. If you want to hide the cord ends of a macramé bracelet, melted nylon is easier to finish off and provides a cleaner looking result than jute or hemp, which produce frayed ends. Synthetic fabrics are strong and hold up to wear and tear compared to a fiber like silk or cotton that might wear out over time. Synthetic fabrics give you more options than natural fabrics do when creating bright, bold, funky designs with a modern twist.

Your local craft or fabric store will carry a wide array of natural and synthetic fabrics. But also search thrift shops, yard sales, or antique shops for fabric, ribbon, and fibers you can use in your jewelry designs. Remember that nothing is off limits; sometimes the most surprising item will provide inspiration for a great jewelry design.

○ cords and threads ○

Cords and fibers are fundamental materials in textile and fiber jewelry design, from threads that bind elements together to knotted cords that provide decoration. Soft fibers can be substituted for traditional jewelry findings—a twisted ribbon or cord might unify your design better than a metal chain, for example—and are available in every imaginable material, texture, and color.

Cords

Although the cord is functional and meant to support the jewelry elements for wearing, it is also decorative. Choose cords that compliment your design in color, scale, and texture. If you want to emphasize the cord, select a cord that is opposite (or complimentary to) your other materials, or pick a neutral cord to contrast with a bright bead. If you want the cord to blend or recede into the design, choose a color in the same hue as the rest of the elements, which will provide a subtle rhythm to the piece.

Thread

Thread is a fundamental supply for virtually all the jewelry projects, whether it is common all-purpose sewing thread or a specialty thread, such as quilting or button thread, for a specific purpose. All-purpose sewing thread is commonly available in virtually every color, shade, and hue to match any fabric. It is a good all-purpose fiber for hand or machine stitching. Quilting or button thread is extra strong and is good to use in places where strength is needed, for example when sewing on clasps. Clear nylon thread is both strong and versatile. It is invisible and provides a way to make attachments without detracting from the design.

Bees wax and thread conditioner help keep thread from tangling or knotting as you work, and are especially helpful when sewing on buttons or charms to fabric.

Other cords and fibers that are both functional and decorative include twisted cord, ribbon yarn, embroidery floss, elastic, and worsted yarn. A wide variety of fibers and cords appropriate for jewelry making fill the shelves of yarn and knit shops to the delight of any creative fiber artist.

beads and buttons

Beads and buttons provide decoration as well as functionality to beautifully finished jewelry pieces. Buttons with shanks on the back make excellent closures, as do larger beads. They can be attached with contrasting or complementary-colored thread to provide yet another design element.

Beads

Small seed beads will add sparkle to the edges of delicately crocheted flowers. Equally appealing, large bold beads can become the focal point when strung creatively along a piece. Make sure you test threads and needles to make sure they will fit through the beads you select. Small beads require fine bead needles and thread to accommodate stringing, while cords sometimes require a large-holed bead. Beads with large holes, commonly made of glass, ceramic, or wood, are harder to come by, but can be found in some bead shops. You can also make your own polymer clay beads if you can't find the right color or style to fit your design. Beads tie the whole piece together, so when choosing a bead for a project, consider its finish and color—does it compliment the fiber? Does it match the style of the project? Though this process may take time, when you finally find the perfect bead for a piece, it's exhilarating. You can jazz up bead designs by layering them with other embellishments such as gems, jewels, or sequins.

Buttons

Buttons with loop shanks on the back are one of my favorite "findings" for making closures for bracelets and necklaces. They are extremely easy to attach—simply slip the cord or fiber through the loop shank, then knot the cord on the other side to attach the button to the cord. Shop for buttons with large enough shanks to accommodate the desired cord or fiber. Antique buttons often have large wire shanks that are perfect for jewelry button closures.

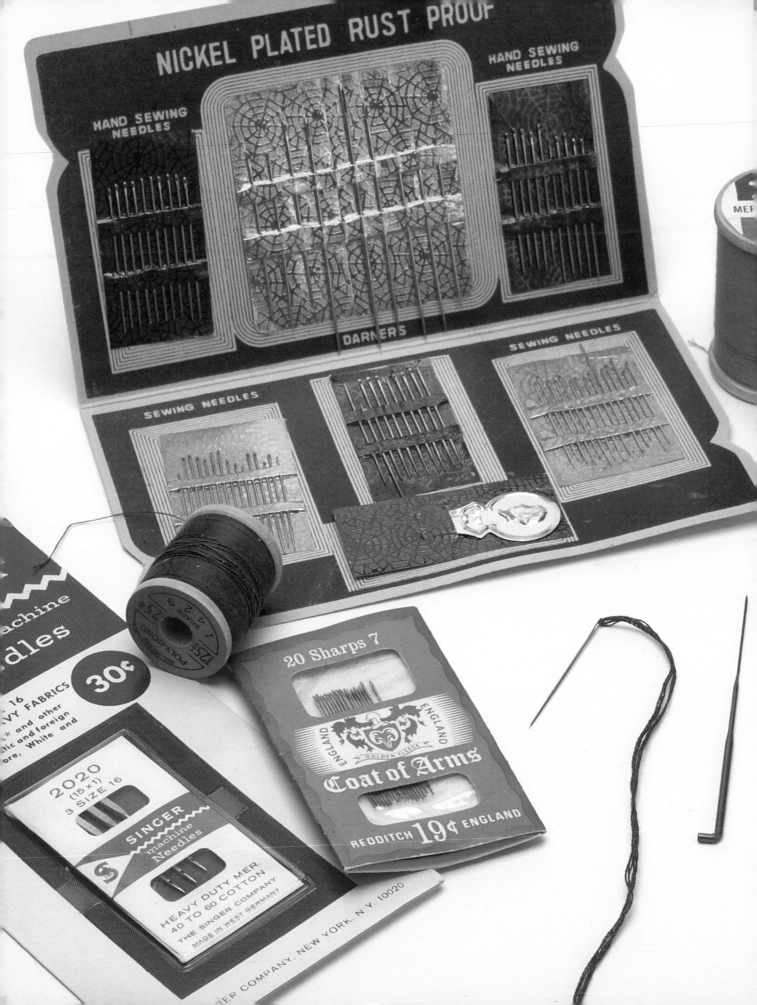

General Supplies and Tools

MOST OF THE SUPPLIES and tools you'll need for the jewelry projects in this book are already in your sewing box or craft drawer. The basics include adhesives, good fabric scissors, handsewing needles, and hooks.

○ adhesives and sealants ○

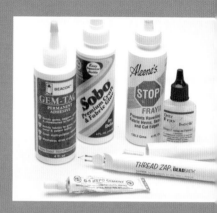

Craft and fabric stores carry a variety of adhesives and fabric sealants especially designed for textiles and fibers. Each product has particular properties designed to work well with these materials. Most types are designed to dry clear and do not discolor the fibers. Be sure to test the adhesive on a scrap piece if in doubt.

White Craft Glues: Thick white glue such as The Ultimate Glue by Crafter's Pick or Sobo glue are all-purpose craft glues that are thick enough to adhere fabric, suede, and felt pieces together. They work well because the glue does not soak or bleed into the fabric or fibers, which gives you control and good adhesion. The glue also dries clear.

Fabric Glue: This adhesive is designed for fabric and ribbon. Manufacturers offer formulations specifically for the type of material to be used including felt, leather, or fabric, which takes the guesswork out of trying to find the right glue for the job.

Gem and Jewel Glues: Gem glue is designed to attach gems, buttons, charms, and beads to porous surfaces such as fabric. Gem-Tac is a favorite product because it holds well and dries clear.

Hem Sealants: Fray Check is a sealant that provides an invisible barrier to prevent fraying of ribbon, cord, or fabric. Other clear drying fabric glues can also be used to prevent frays.

Iron-On Adhesive: Double-sided, heat-activated adhesive is perfect for bonding fabric elements such as appliqués. Therm O Web makes several products with varying bond strengths, depending on the type of fabric used.

Jewelry Cements: This clear adhesive is available in fine-tipped applicator tubes to provide a tidy finish for delicate cord ends or tight areas where just a tiny dot of glue is required.

Heat Tools: Although not a glue, heat will seal synthetic fabrics and cord ends. Thread-Zap by Bead Smith is a battery-operated wax-melting tool that has a fine tip designed to melt and seal the ends of nylon cord. The Creative Textile Tool is a versatile tool with interchangable tips that offer various ways to melt and seal fibers, such as ribbon.

○ cutting tools ○

Having the right scissors and cutting tools will make a big difference as you create fabric projects. Fabric scissors are specifically designed to cut fabric and will help you trim cleanly around curves and pattern shapes. Don't use fabric scissors for heavy cord or other hard-to-cut materials; they will dull the blades. Instead, use inexpensive household scissors. Small pointed embroidery scissors are good for clipping threads and for cutting in tight areas.

Rotary cutters, designed for quiltmaking, make it a snap to cut straight lines or strips of fabric. Always use a quilting ruler and self-healing mat in conjunction with the rotary cutter.

For a fancy edge, use pinking shears on ribbon or fabric. They also help prevent fraying for a neat edge.

A Japanese screw punch is a bookbinder's tool that cuts clean holes in fabric, just as it does in paper. Be sure to put an old phone book or magazine behind the work as you punch, as it cuts easily all the way through all layers with minimal effort.

◦ needles ◦

For many of the projects in the book, hand sewing is required. A standard sewing needle with all-purpose sewing thread will be sufficient for most projects. When working with embroidery floss or craft thread, use an embroidery needle. Needles with large eyes and blunt tips such as tapestry or darning needles are good for heavier threads, elastic, or yarn. A larger needle is also helpful for turning and forming corners and in other tight areas. In contrast to larger needles, beading needles are very fine and are good for stringing and sewing small seed beads to a project. They are

available in two types: a flexible, twisted wire with a collapsible eye (used exclusively for stringing), or, a thin needle that looks just like a traditional sewing needle, but is much finer and has a smaller eye (used for both stringing and sewing). Felting needles are specialty needles made for felting wool; they are very sharp with barbs on the shaft of the needle. Take care when using this or any other sharp tool.

◦ hooks ◦

A number of projects in this book require a hook, primarily a crochet hook. The size hook you'll need is determined by the weight of the fiber used or the gauge of the finished work. Smaller hooks will create tightly woven stitches, and large hooks produce larger open stitches. Yarn shops carry a wide variety of hooks. It's nice to have a set with multiple sizes so you will always have the right hook for the fiber you are using.

A rug hook looks similar to a crochet hook, but has a handle on the end, which a crochet hook does not. (A rug hook is used in the Hooked Fabric Flowers project on page 33.)

○ other tools and supplies ○

You'll also need some basic sewing and common home office supplies for the projects, all of which you are very likely to have on hand.

Fabric Pens and Pencils: Fabric/quilting pens and pencils will dissolve or fade from fabric and are used for temporary markings. They are great for tracing patterns or drawing embroidery designs on fabric. Use dark colors for drawing on light fabrics or white or yellow for drawing on dark fabrics. A permanent marker is handy for marking bold lines, when needed. But remember that these markers do not wash out or fade, so don't use them anywhere that they might show in your finished piece.

Sewing Supplies: In addition to needles, thread, and scissors, some basic sewing supplies such as a tape measure, ruler, pins, and seam ripper (in case you make a mistake) will all be helpful to have on hand for your fabric and fiber jewelry projects.

Binder Clips: Binder clips from the office supply store are perfect for holding pieces together while glue dries, or for holding cord in place while braiding or knotting macramé.

○ jewelry findings and pliers ○

A few basic findings (or jewelry parts) and tools are used consistently throughout the projects in the book. Using the right tools and findings will give your work a professional finish.

Findings

Findings are the parts used to assemble jewelry, such as clasps, pin backs, and jump rings. They come in many sizes and finishes, and you should select your findings to enhance your jewelry designs.

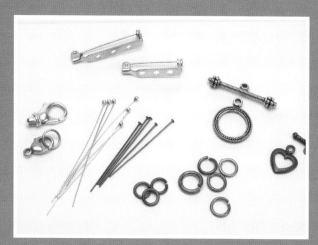

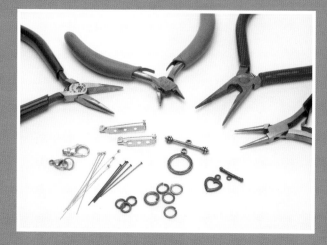

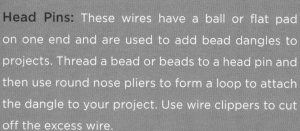

Head Pins: These wires have a ball or flat pad on one end and are used to add bead dangles to projects. Thread a bead or beads to a head pin and then use round nose pliers to form a loop to attach the dangle to your project. Use wire clippers to cut off the excess wire.

Pin Backs: These are available in silver or gold colors (usually base metal) and come in varying lengths depending on the size needed for the finished project. They can be attached either by sewing in place or gluing to the back of the finished pin.

Clasps: Bead shops and variety stores carry clasps for jewelry making. I prefer either lobster clasps or a loop-and-toggle style. A lobster clasp is nice to use because on many designs all you need to do is make a loop on one end of the necklace or bracelet and then attach a single lobster clasp to the other end to complete the closure. I like loop-

and-toggle closures because they are easy to link (especially one-handed for bracelets), and they are very stylish. Choose a clasp that works with your design, taking the scale, finish, and shape of the clasp in to consideration to find the perfect one.

Jump Rings: These are small metal rings that are used to link components together. These are available in base metal or in gold or silver at bead shops. For a stronger jump ring, look for a heavier-gauge wire, and keep in mind the scale of your project.

To open jump rings: Twist the ends out sideways with pliers; don't pull them apart. Opening the jump rings the wrong way adds stress to the metal. Close them in the same fashion as you opened them, bring the ends back together moving them sideways until they scrape together and touch in the middle (see page 64, step 13).

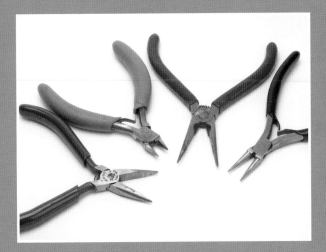

Pliers

Pliers are essential hand tools for jewelry making. They are made with a variety of jaw configurations, and each jaw type facilitates specific techniques. You will need a few basic types for professional results. Pliers are used to form wire loops, attach jump rings, and for gripping and crimping. Jeweler's pliers do not have teeth on the jaw because they are designed to bend and move metal wire without marring the metal's surface. Also be sure to have wire cutters close at hand to clip finished wire ends.

Round-nose Pliers: These pliers are used to form loops with wire; the tips of the pliers are graduated for making loops of various sizes.

Chain-nose Pliers: The pliers are used to open and close jump rings. They are also used to grip the wire and hold it in place as you twist, wrap, or make connections with the wire. These are good all-purpose pliers for a variety of jewelry making techniques.

Needle-nose Pliers: Needle-nose pliers are similar to chain-nose pliers except that the needle-nose varieties have teeth that grip. I use these pliers to

pull a cord or wire through a stubborn bead. They are common household pliers you may already own. Any hardware store will carry them.

Wire Cutters: A good pair of quality wire cutters will cut wire neatly, especially when cutting close to a wire wrap. Reserve good jewelry cutters for fine gauge wires. Use inexpensive heavy-duty cutters from the hardware store for heavy-gauge wire that would otherwise dull or even ruin your good jewelry cutters.

PROJECTS

No-sew

YOU DON'T HAVE TO KNOW how to sew to make accessories out of fabric. With the advent of modern adhesives and fabric glues, it's easy to work with pieces and strips of fabric to create wrapped or layered elements to use in jewelry designs.

fabric-covered bead necklace

THIS IS a great no-sew project that features batik dyed fabric strips (i.e., bias-cut fabric fiber). This necklace would look great when paired with cotton or linen fabric, perfect for a casual summer party or any time you want a great accessory with a soft, earthy look.

MATERIALS & SUPPLIES

Mirah's Crafts Batik Ribbon Yarn in garnet and ruby (Alternatively, you can cut your own bias fabric strips; ½ to ¾ yards of fabric will produce all the strips you need.)

Large wooden craft beads with big holes, eight to ten as desired

White glue

Toothpicks

Large-eye needle (to accommodate fabric strips and cord)

Cord for stringing, medium-to-heavy novelty fiber, 3 yards

Two small wooden beads for cord ends

1. Cut off a long strip of fiber (about a yard for a large bead). Use a toothpick to apply white glue just inside the hole of the bead.

2. While the glue is wet, use the toothpick to push the end of the fiber into the hole. Roll the toothpick over the fabric inside the bead to adhere it smoothly to the inside of the bead.

3. Apply a straight, thin line of glue halfway around the bead, from hole to hole.

4. Wrap the fiber strip around the bead, over the glue, smoothing with your fingers.

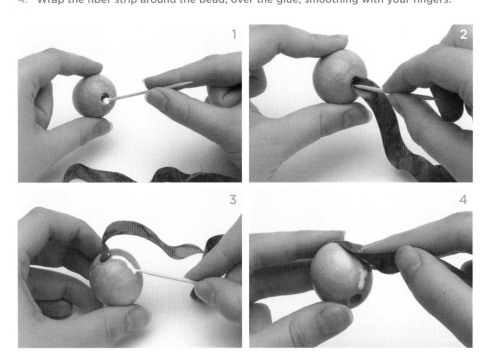

5. Thread the end of the fiber strip into a large-eyed needle. Using the needle to feed the fiber strip through the bead hole, pull the strip completely through the hole until the strip is taut.

6. Continue wrapping around the outside of the bead, threading the fiber strip through the hole with each wrap. Lightly glue and slightly overlap the edges with each wrap until the entire bead is covered.

7. Cut off and tuck the end of the fiber into the hole, gluing it in place after the last wrap. Use the toothpick to push the end of the last fiber strip neatly inside the hole. Wipe off any excess glue with a damp cloth and let the bead dry. Repeat until you've made eight to ten beads, or as many as you'd like in your necklace.

8. You can now string the beads on the cord. I used a double cord, but you can use a single cord if you prefer. For the double cord, cut two 1½-yard lengths of cord. Thread the two ends of the cords into a large-eyed needle. Pull the needle and doubled cord through the bead's hole, sliding the bead along the cords to the desired position. To secure the bead in position, wrap the cord on the outside of the bead and back through the opposite hole. Repeat until all beads are strung, adjusting bead positions along the cord as desired. To create the closure, secure the cord near the ends with a wrapped finishing knot (see page 111), which will allow you to adjust the length of the necklace. Add small beads to the ends of the cord, knotting at the base of each to finish the ends. Use white glue to seal the cord ends.

hooked fabric flowers

Project by **Mary Stanley**

RUG HOOKING involves pulling a series of loops through a backing fabric such as burlap. This craft was made popular in the 1800s by craftspeople in New England. Mary is known for her beautiful folk art designs, which she achieves through her use of hand-dyed wool, recycled fabrics, and beautiful color combinations.

MATERIALS & SUPPLIES

Strips of felted wool, silk, or rayon, ¼- to ⅜-inch wide x 12 to 18 inches long (eight to ten strips per flower, depending on length of strips) in colors of your choice

Burlap or monk's cloth, 8-inches square (to fit small embroidery hoop)

Embroidery hoop, small

Permanent marker

Rug hook

Ultimate Craft Glue (Crafter's Pick) or another clear-drying white fabric glue

Ribbon for leaves, 1 inch to 1½ inches x 6 inches

Handsewing needle and all-purpose thread or a few strands of embroidery floss

Fabric scissors

Drinking glass or lid for circle template

Pin back

Small circle of felt for pin back, any color

1. Cut a piece of burlap large enough to fit in your embroidery hoop. Using the marker, draw a circle the size of your finished flower on the burlap. (A round glass or lid makes a good template.) Cut or tear eight to ten ¼- to ⅜-inch strips of assorted wool or other fabric to use for flower.

2. Hold the hook in your dominant hand and the first strip under the burlap with your other hand. Insert the hook into the center of the drawn circle and pull about 1 inch of the tail of the strip through the burlap.

3. You will work out from the center in a spiral or circular pattern of hooked loops to form the flower. (The ends will be cut later to match the height of the pile.) For the first hooked loop, insert the hook down into the burlap, close to the tail that was pulled through in Step 1. Hook the strip from the under side of the burlap and pull the loop through to the top side, using your hand on the under side to hold and guide the strip as you pull the loop through. Pull the loop to the top until it is about ¼ inch in height. Continue hooking loops from the back, working from the center out. Hook the loops fairly close together for a "fuller" flower.

4. When you are ready to change colors or come to the end of a strip, pull the end of the strip through to the front and trim it to about 1 inch long. To start a new strip, hook the new strip through the same hole as the end of the previous strip (you will have two ends showing right next to each other as shown in the photo).

5. Begin to form loops with the new strip, following the instructions in Steps 3 and 4.

6. Continue hooking loops in a spiral progression, changing colors as desired until the loops fill the circle. Finish by pulling the end of the last strip up to the top side and clip.

7. Cut around the finished flower, leaving a ½-inch border of unfinished burlap around the edge.

8. Apply thick glue to the burlap border on the under side of the work.

9. Fold the edges of the burlap border in toward the center, gathering the burlap and gluing in place.

10. To make the leaves, fold the ends of a piece of ribbon as shown, forming a point at the fold.

11. Stitch across the base of the leaf through all thicknesses with a running stitch to gather. Cut off the excess ribbon below the stitching and pull to lightly gather and shape.

12. If desired, sew a decorative "vein" down the center of the leaf using a backstitch.

13. Glue the leaf or leaves into place on the back of the flower.

14. Stitch a pin back to a small piece of felt for the back of the pin. Glue the felt to the back of the flower to complete the pin.

Sewing and Quilting

HAND SEWING with a needle and thread is a fundamental skill that some purists insist on for a vintage-inspired "handmade" piece. Others prefer to use machine stitching to create sewn items such as a pieced quilted design. For either method, be sure to choose good needles and the proper thread for insured success.

ribbon flower pins

STRIPED GROSGRAIN is available in a variety of cheery colors to make festive flower pins. A heated tool is used to cut a soft, flowing edge along the ribbon, which gives the flower petals an organic, naturalistic feel. Flower stamens are commonly found wherever bridal supplies are sold. (Vintage pieces make especially beautiful centers.) Check the Suppliers section on page 126 for more information.

MATERIALS & SUPPLIES

1¹⁄₂- to 2-inch wide striped grosgrain ribbon (Strano Designs), one 18-inch length per flower, or any wide grosgrain ribbon

Creative Textile Tool with tapered point (Walnut Hollow)

Tempered Glass Mat (Walnut Hollow)

Handsewing needle and thread (all-purpose, quilting, or button)

Artificial flower stamens or wired beads for flower centers

Floral wire, 24 or 26 gauge, 8 inches

Ultimate Craft Glue (Crafter's Pick) or another thick, white fabric glue

Pin back

Piece of felt for pin back

1. Cut an 18-inch length of ribbon for the flower. Place the ribbon on the glass mat and pre-heat the textile tool with the tapered point attached. Hold the ribbon with your non-dominant hand as you melt and cut the ribbon with the tool. The heat of the tool melts the ribbon, which seals the fibers as it cuts. Cut a soft wave pattern along the length of the ribbon, as shown. This particular ribbon is wide enough to make two flowers (one with each half of the ribbon). Taper off at the end to avoid a squared off edge.

2. With a doubled thread knotted at the end, sew a long basting stitch about ¹⁄₄ inch from the straight edge of the ribbon. Pull basting thread to evenly gather the ribbon.

3. Starting at one end of the ribbon, coil the ribbon tightly into a circle and tack with the needle and thread. Working on the wrong (back) side, spiral (or coil) the ribbon, tacking the ribbon as you go. Each rotation will overlap the last slightly to build the flower shape.

4. Adjust the gathers as you go, stitching the ribbon in place as you coil to the end of the ribbon. When the entire length of ribbon is coiled, knot and clip the thread ends.

5. Use floral wire to gather and wrap around purchased artificial stamens for the flower center. (Or, you can use beads on wire for the center.) Push the stamens into the center of the ribbon flower and secure them with glue.

6. Stitch a pin back to a small piece of felt for the back of the pin. Glue the felt to the back of the flower to complete the pin.

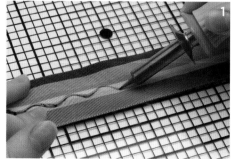

yo-yo necklace

YO-YOS are little circles of fabric gathered around the edges, which are then sewn together. They are most often associated with quilt making. Yo-yo quilts made from colorful fabric scraps were particularly popular in the 1930s and 1940s. Yo-yos are easy to make, and this necklace adds elegant designer fabrics, buttons, and beads to a retro-inspired piece.

MATERIALS & SUPPLIES

Assorted scraps of coordinating fabrics of any fiber content or type.

Cardboard (cereal boxes work well) for three yo-yo templates, 4 inches x 8 inches or larger

Drinking glass or lid for circle template

Fabric marking pencil

Handsewing needle and all-purpose thread

Buttons, pearls, and beads for embellishment

Chain, any style or size

Clasp, any style or size to fit chain

1. To make the yo-yo template, trace around the glass or lid onto a piece of cardboard. Make different size templates, ranging from 2 inches to 3½ inches in diameter. Cut templates. Trace around the templates with a fabric marking pencil on the wrong side of the fabric, varying the sizes of the circles.

2. Cut out the various fabric circles.

3. Fold the edge of each circle over about ⅛ inch to the wrong side of the fabric, finger pressing as you go for a neater finish. Using strong quilting or button thread (doubled and knotted), baste stitch around the entire edge of the yo-yo to gather.

4. Pull the thread to gather the fabric into the center of the yo-yo.

5. Pull the basting thread tightly, tie a knot in the center, and clip the thread.

6. String or sew the yo-yos together to make a bracelet, necklace, or use alone as a pin. To make stacked yo-yos, layer smaller yo-yos on top of larger ones. Stitch through the center of both yo-yos to attach them.

7. Stitch beads or buttons to the center of the stack.

8. To secure the beads and buttons, knot the thread in the center on the back of the larger yo-yo. Bring the needle and thread back up through the yo-yo stack and knot again to hide the end of the thread. Clip the thread.

9. Sew the stacked yo-yos together, attaching them side by side with a needle and thread. Sew together as many as you like for your design. Tip: When stitching the yo-yos side by side, stitch them slightly higher than the mid-point on each side so that they won't flip over when worn.

10. After you have stitched the all the yo-yo stacks together, sew a length of chain to each end, adjusting the length to achieve your desired finished length. Add a clasp to the ends of the chain.

mixed media fabric charms

THIS BRACELET is a fun project for an organized swap. Invite a group of friends to make fabric charms to exchange. Choose a theme (nature, music, holidays) or leave it wide open. You'll all end up with a variety of charms to back to hang on your bracelets, each as unique as the person who lovingly made it.

MATERIALS & SUPPLIES

Fabric scraps including muslin and various solids and prints, each cut about 2 inches x 2 inches square

Pellon fusible fleece

Fabrico fabric stamp pads

Stamps, any stamps at all

Inkjet linen fabric sheets (The Vintage Workshop)

Vintage art CD or downloadable images (The Vintage Workshop)

Seed beads (any color or style) for embellishing

Japanese screw punch

Sewing machine and standard sewing machine needles

Handsewing needle

Fabric scissors

All-purpose thread

Chopstick (optional)

Eyelets, 1/8 inch, about ten

Hammer, eyeletsetter, and mat

White fabric glue

Finished bracelet chain (any type of purchased chain) or make your own, to fit wrist

Jump rings, 8–10mm or any large jump ring, enough rings for charms, plus extras for dangles

Pliers

Iron and ironing board

1. Cut fabric or muslin into 2-inch squares. Using stamps and stamp pads, stamp designs onto the fabric. These will be used for the fronts and backs of the charms and to embellish them.

2. Print images onto inkjet linen following manufacturer's instructions. Cut out printed designs, and peel off the backing from the printed fabric.

3. Choose pairs of printed fabrics for the charms. Place the selected pairings right sides together and draw round, heart, or square shapes on the wrong side of each pair with a pencil. Be sure to center your designs. Machine stitch (or hand sew) directly along the pencil lines, leaving a small opening to turn the shapes right side out later. Cut a shape of fusible fleece that is slightly smaller than the inside of the stitching line and iron in place. Trim around the entire shape leaving a 1/8-inch seam allowance.

4. For heart and round shapes, clip around the curves and for square shapes, clip corners before turning.

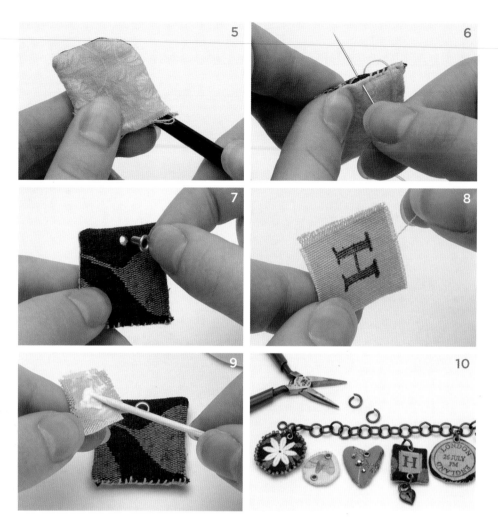

5. Turn the shape right side out. Use a chopstick, or another thin, dull point to shape corners and tight spots after turning. Press flat if necessary.

6 Turn the raw edge of the opening to the inside and hand stitch the opening shut.

7. Fit a Japanese screw punch with a punch to fit the eyelet size. Punch a hole for hanging the charm through all layers of fabric. (Use an old magazine as a work surface for hole punching.) Push an eyelet through the hole, as shown. Hammer the eyelet with a setter on an eyelet-setting mat. Tap the finished eyelet to flatten slightly on the fabric.

8. Fray the edge of a smaller stamped piece of fabric that will be applied to the finished charm.

9. Finish the charms by gluing on fabric, rhinestones, or other decorative elements. Glue the stamped fabric shapes to the front side of the charms.

10. Stitch seed beads around the edges of some of the charms. Use pliers to attach the charms to a finished chain with jump rings.

quilted cuff

Project by **Rachel Haab**

A PIECED QUILT, designed in miniature, creates a simple cuff-style bracelet. If piecework isn't your cup of tea try incorporating elaborate crazy quilt designs with embroidered and dimensional embellishments, appliqué shapes stitched on a background fabric, or cut the shape of the cuff with an asymmetrical border to add interest.

Materials & Supplies

Scraps of assorted fabric, at least three or more coordinating colors

Pellon fusible fleece 24-inch piece of ribbon, any kind

Handsewing needle

All-purpose thread

Sequins and beads for embellishment

Fabric scissors

Rotary cutter and cutting mat

See-through ruler

Sewing machine and regular sewing machine needle

Iron and ironing board

Sewing pins

1. Measure your wrist to determine the finished size of the bracelet. Add $\frac{1}{2}$ inch to the length and width of that measurement to allow for a $\frac{1}{2}$-inch seam allowance. Cut out fabric scraps in varying lengths and widths (these will be sewn together to create the cuff). This is a free-form design, so the pieces can vary in shape and size. Keep the strips at least long enough to give you plenty of room to trim the bracelet width later.

2. Sew the fabric scraps together using a $\frac{1}{4}$-inch seam allowance for all seams. (Some of the strips consist of shorter pieces that are sewn together vertically.)

3. Press the seam allowances and trim to $\frac{1}{4}$ inch, if necessary. Lay the sewn-together fabric band down on a cutting mat and trim to the measurements in Step 1 (wrist measurement plus $\frac{1}{2}$-inch seam allowance), using a rotary cutter and see-through ruler.

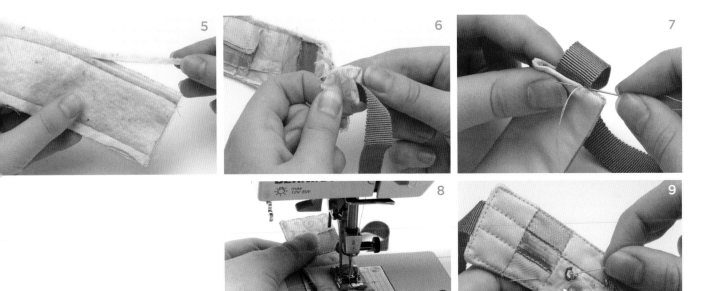

Cut a solid piece of fabric and a piece of fusible fleece the same size as the band for the reverse side of the bracelet. Iron the fleece to the wrong side of the solid fabric.

4. Cut two 12-inch lengths of ribbon for the ties. Lay one piece of ribbon down the center length of the solid fabric on the right side of the fabric. Lap the ribbon just a little bit over the short raw edge to ensure it will be stitched into the seam (one end of the ribbon will be stitched to the short edge of the fabric and the other end left free). With right sides facing, place the pieced fabric on top of the solid fabric. (The ribbon is sandwiched between these two fabric layers.) Pin the fabric layers together, keeping the loose end of the ribbon free.

5. Machine stitch a $1/4$-inch seam around three sides, leaving one end open for turning the bracelet right side out. (The open end is the end with the loose ribbon.) Trim all seams close to the stitching and clip the corners.

6. Turn the bracelet right side out and press.

7. On the open side of the bracelet, turn the raw edges inward and press. Center the ribbon in between the two layers and pin. Slipstitch the two edges together, going through the ribbon. Knot and hide the thread tails inside the bracelet.

8. Quilt the bracelet by stitching on the face of the bracelet, backstitching at both ends to secure the thread. Edgestitch around the perimeter of the bracelet.

9. To add beads and sequins, thread the needle and hide the knot under a sequin or large bead. Handsew sequins and beads to the quilted surface, making sure that you only go through the top layer of fabric, keeping the back of the bracelet neat. When finished, hide the last knot under a sequin and hide the thread tails within the bracelet.

Embroidery and Appliqué

BASIC EMBROIDERY stitches and appliqué techniques provide a myriad of possibilities for jewelry design. Use brightly-colored embroidery threads to add dimension and contrast to your projects. Embroidery stitches can also be functional. Use them to create attachments or to finish the raw edges of a piece.

embroidery stitches

EMBROIDERY is the art of decorating fabric with various hand stitches. Use an embroidery needle with traditional embroidery floss, or choose another type of thread as indicated in the instructions. Add beads or sequins for extra sparkle and dimension. If you are a novice at embroidery, or, if you need a refresher on the basics, practice the appropriate stitches before beginning a project.

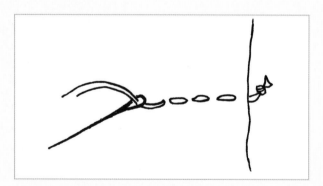

RUNNING OR BASTING STITCH

Anchor the thread on the wrong side of the fabric. Bring the needle through to the right side of the fabric, then back down through to the wrong side, as shown, keeping even spaces between equally-sized stitches.

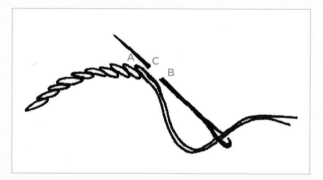

STEM STITCH

Work from left to right. Anchor the thread on the wrong side of the fabric and bring the needle through to the right side (A). Insert the needle at point B at a slight angle. Exit at point C. Note that B is slightly below the stitching line and C is slightly above, which gives a slant, or angle, to the stitch. Make subsequent stitches the same way, keeping stitches close together.

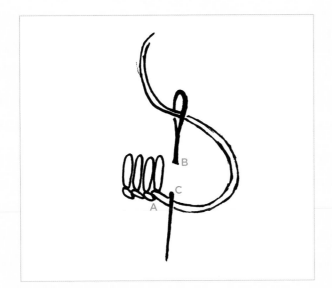

A to B should be equal to the distance from from A to C. Repeat the same stitch again starting at point C to make an unbroken line of stitches. Finish by bringing the thread and needle to the back of the work and knot to secure.

BLANKET STITCH

Work from left to right. Anchor the thread on the wrong side of the fabric and bring the needle through to the right side (A). Keeping the thread *under* the needle and the needle pointing toward you, insert the needle vertically through the fabric from B to C. Draw the needle and thread through the thread loop, and pull the thread taut, forming a small horizontal stitch at the bottom of the vertical stitch, as shown. Make successive stitches the same way.

FRENCH KNOT

Anchor the thread on the wrong side of the fabric then bring the needle through to the right side. Hold the thread down with the non-working thumb and wrap the thread around the needle two times. Keep holding the thread firmly as you insert the needle back in, next to the point where the thread emerged. Pull thread through to the wrong side and secure (for one knot) or move on to the next knot.

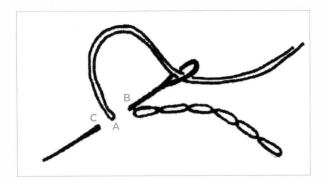

EVEN BACKSTITCH

Work from right to left. Anchor the thread on the wrong side of the fabric then bring the needle through the fabric to the right side (A). Insert the needle at point B and exit at C. The distance from

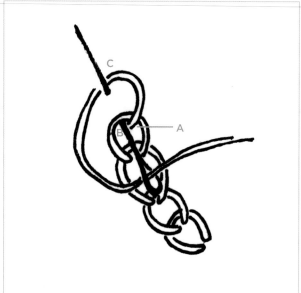

CHAIN STITCH

Working from the wrong side of the fabric bring the needle up through the fabric to the right side (A). Reinsert the needle down into the fabric, right next to where you came up (B). Do not pull the thread taut, instead leave a small loop on the surface of the fabric. Holding the loop down with your nonworking thumb, bring the needle up to the right side, through the loop keeping the thread taut, but not too tight (C). Repeat to form a chain of stitches (note that C becomes A for new chain stitch). When you are finished with the chain, insert the needle on the other side of the loop and secure on the wrong side of fabric.

LAZY DAISY STITCH

This stitch is worked the same way as a chain stitch, except each stitch (loop) is fastened with a small stitch at the top. Begin at the center of your flower. Anchor the thread on the wrong side of the fabric and bring the needle through to the right side. With the needle pointing away from you, insert the needle (the length of the petal) next to where the anchor thread emerges. Loop the thread, counter clockwise, under the needle (A). Insert the needle just above the loop, and make a small stitch at the top of the loop (B), forming the petal. Return to the center point of the daisy to make each subsequent stitch.

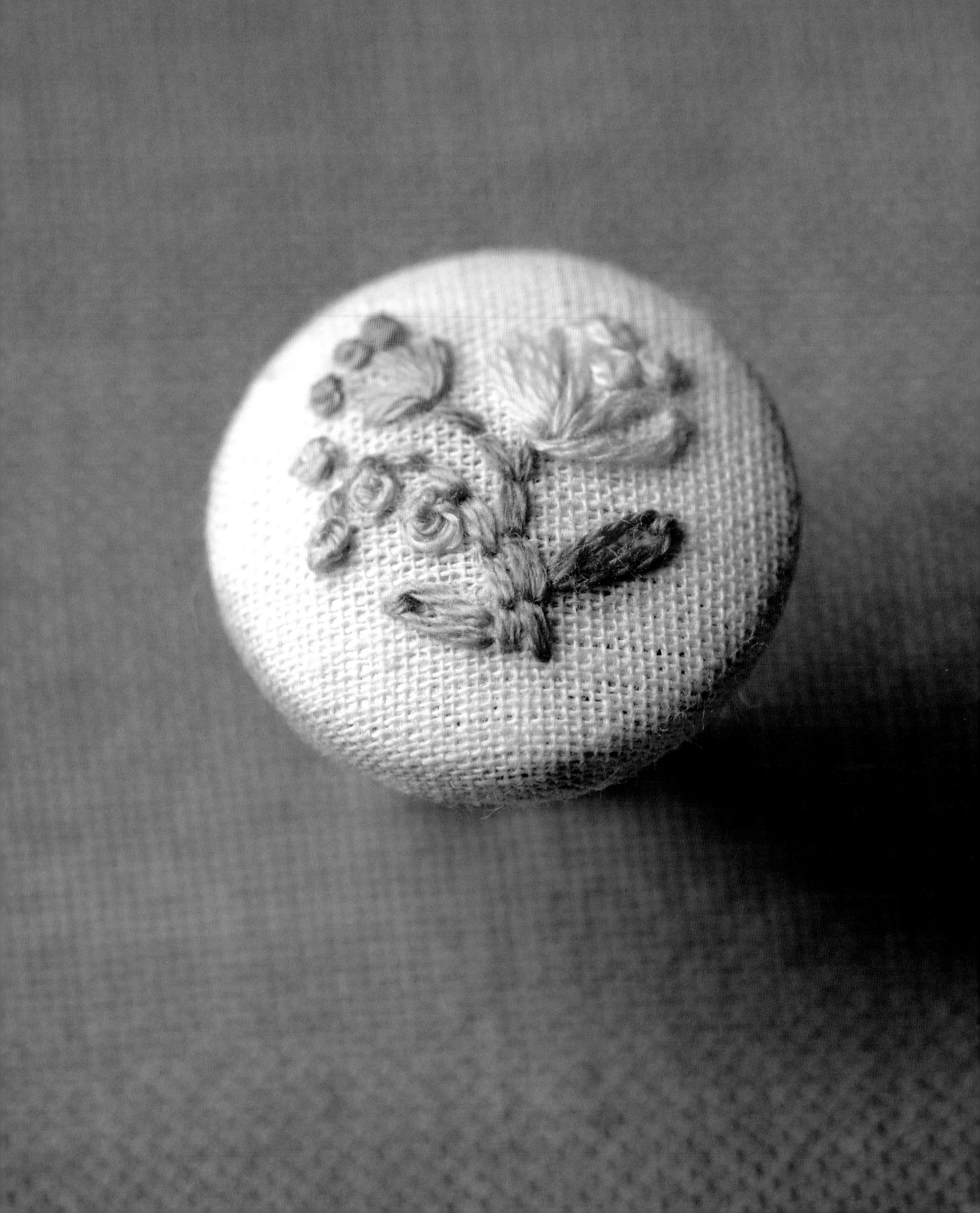

embroidered rings

Project by **Rachel Haab**

EMBROIDERY projects need not be complicated. These rings only use a few simple embroidery stitches and are a departure from making tablecloths or pillowcases. For variation you can make ponytail holders by attaching elastic bands to the backs instead of ring findings.

MATERIALS & SUPPLIES

Small pieces of cotton or muslin fabric, large enough to fit button blanks

Embroidery floss, any color(s)

Embroidery needle

Covered Button Kit (Dritz)

Pliers, chain or needlenose

2-part epoxy adhesive (Devcon 2-ton epoxy resin)

Adjustable ring blanks (sherrihaab.com)

Fine beading needle, thread (optional)

Seed beads (optional)

1   Sketch designs onto muslin or other chosen fabric. Embroider designs with colored embroidery floss following diagrams for various stitches (see pages 54 to 56). Cut fabric into circles to fit the covered buttons, centering the embroidered design and using the pattern included in the button kit. (If the fabric is thin, cut two layers of fabric to prevent the metal button from showing through.) Remove the shank from the back of the button by pinching it with pliers.

2. Baste stitch around the edge of the fabric circle to gather the fabric to fit around the button; do not knot the thread.

3. Center the fabric over the button (with embroidery design right side up) and pull the basting thread to gather the fabric around the button tightly.

4. Knot and clip the thread after the fabric is pulled tight around the button.

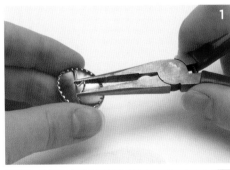

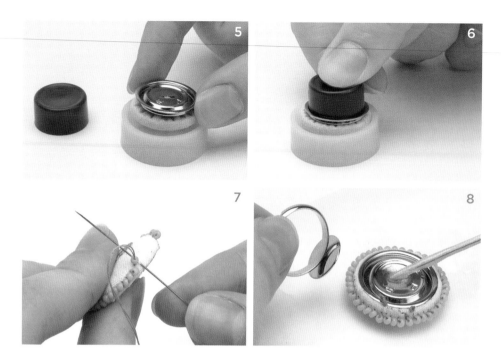

5. Place the finished button right side down in the center of the mold/setter, which comes in the kit. Place the backplate over the button.

6. Press down firmly with the pusher (also in the kit) until the backplate snaps into place.

7. Use a fine beading needle and all-purpose thread to stitch seed beads around the edge of the button, if desired.

8. Mix equal parts of two-part epoxy on wax paper. Apply the epoxy to the back of the button and attach it to the ring blank. Keep the ring level, and let the epoxy dry overnight.

embellished appliqué necklace

APPLIQUÉ is the technique of stitching cut-out shapes to a foundation fabric and is commonly used in quilting. This asymmetrical, bohemian-style necklace features colorful images cut from fabric and then appliquéd to create charming dangles. The dangles can be made from long-forgotten fabric odds and ends from your sewing or craft supply box. Be creative and don't be afraid to incorporate unusual items to add texture and color.

MATERIALS & SUPPLIES

Printed cotton fabric with small patterns or designs, which can be cut out for the appliqués

Heavy muslin fabric, 1/8 yard or small scraps

Ultrasuede, 1/8 yard or small scraps

Handsewing needle

Strong quilting or button thread

Scissors

Pinking shears

DMC Craft Thread or embroidery floss or for appliqué stitching

Embroidery needle

Therm O Web HeatnBond®

Lite The Ultimate Craft Glue (Crafter's Pick)

Sequins, seed beads or other small objects for embellishing fabric pieces

Japanese screw punch with size 3mm hole

1/8-inch eyelets, four to five

Eyelet setter

Hammer

Mat for setting eyelets

Jump rings, about ten 3/4-inch plastic cabone rings

Head pins

Size 5 cotton crochet thread, red or color to coordinate with fabrics

Assorted glass or plastic beads to coordinate with fabrics

Round-nose pliers

Long-nose or chain-nose pliers

Iron and ironing board

Fabric marking pen or pencil

Wire cutters

1. Choose a few design elements from your printed fabric—a larger image for the center focal point and a few other smaller designs to complement the center design. Before cutting out the pieces, use iron to fuse the HeatnBond to the wrong side of the fabric. (Follow manufacturer's instructions for details on heat fusing). Allow to cool then peel off the paper.

2. Using scissors, cut out the shapes from the fused fabric prepared in Step 1. Iron the shapes onto a piece of muslin using the cotton setting. This will activate the HeatnBond adhesive.

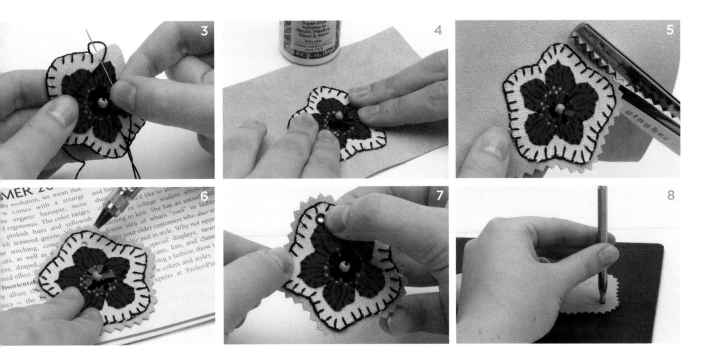

3. Cut out the muslin-fused shapes, leaving a ¼-inch border of muslin around them. Thread a needle with embroidery floss or thread, and blanket stitch around the edges of the muslin and around the edges of the designs themselves (see page 55). Stitch on sequins and seed beads to decorate the pieces. In this example the needle comes up through the center of the sequin, through the seed bead and then back down through the center of the sequin to the back of the fabric to secure. Add other small beads or elements with fabric glue or stitch them onto the fabric as desired. Finish off with a knot on the back of the work.

4. Apply a layer of craft glue to the back (wrong side) of the muslin pieces and adhere to Ultrasuede.

5. Cut around edges of Ultrasued-backed pieces with pinking shears to create a decorative border.

6. The finished fabric pieces will be attached to the chain with eyelets and jump rings. Mark holes for eyelet placement on the finished fabric pieces. Use a Japanese screw punch to make the holes for the eyelets. Place the piece on a magazine (to use as a mat) and push the punch firmly through all fabric layers.

7. Push an eyelet through the hole made in Step 6.

8. Turn the piece over and set it on a mat. Use an eyelet setter and hammer to set the eyelet. Add eyelets in the same manner to all of the cut design pieces. Set the pieces aside.

9. To cover the cabone ring, cut a 36-inch length of crochet thread and fold in half to form a loop. Tie cord to ring using a lark's head knot (see page 109).

10. Tie a series of lark's head sennet knots (see page 109), working in both directions around the ring, tying equal number of knots until both cords meet on the opposite side.

11. Tie alternating half-hitch knots (see page 110) with the ends of the cords until the cords are about 5 inches long.

12. Arrange the knotted cord and the fabric design elements made in Step 8 along the chain to achieve your desired design. Using jump rings through the eyelets, attach the fabric pieces to the chain. Using wire cutters, cut the chain into sections as desired to create a pleasing design. Connect the knotted cabone ring to the chain using a jump ring; tie the ends of the cord to the chain using any knot.

13. Use two pairs of pliers to open and close jump rings, as shown. Tie the cord ends to the chain with lark's head knots. Tie decorative beads to the ends of the cord. Add glass or plastic beads along the chain using head pins and wrapped wire loops; clip off excess wire with wire cutters. Tie bits of fabric or netting for textural elements to embellish the finished necklace.

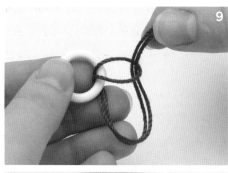

heat-etched velvet and ribbon cuff

VELVET has a unique property in that you can heat and melt the pile away from the backing. For this striking cuff, a fine-tipped heat tool is used like a pen to create a delicate etched design in the velvet. Make a personalized bracelet by etching a name, or draw on your design of choice.

MATERIALS & SUPPLIES

⅝-inch-wide velvet ribbon (acetate/rayon), 9 inches long

White fabric pencil

Creative Textile Tool with long mini flow point tip (Walnut Hollow)

Tempered Glass Mat (Walnut Hollow)

Masking or Scotch tape to temporarily hold ribbon to mat

2-inch wide ribbon or trim to coordinate with velvet ribbon, 9 inches long

Four small pieces of Ultrasuede; cut about 1 inch wide and a little longer than the width of the wider ribbon

2-inch length of cord for closure

Button for closure

Embroidery floss and needle

Fabric scissors

Small beads for embellishment, shell, glass, or plastic

1. Cut a 9-inch length of velvet ribbon. Using a white fabric pencil, write a name or other design on the right (velvet) side of the ribbon. Tape the short ends of the ribbon (¼ inch over the edge) onto the heat-proof glass mat. Heat up the Creative Textile Tool fitted with the long mini flow point. Trace over your penciled design with the tip of the tool to burn away the velvet pile, leaving an etched image on the ribbon. Keep the tool moving, lifting as needed to check your design. (If you leave the tool in one place too long you risk burning through the back of the ribbon.) Remove the tape by trimming off the ends of the ribbon with scissors.

2. Center the wrong side of the etched velvet ribbon on top of the right side of the wider ribbon and machine or handstitch the ribbons together lengthwise down the middle. Cut the ribbon to the desired length for the finished cuff. The cuff will meet end to end on your wrist; it will not overlap. Cut four Ultrasuede pieces to conceal the ends of the ribbon, making sure the Ultrasuede pieces are about 1- to 1½-inch wide and a little longer than the width of the ribbon, as shown. Position pieces of Ultrasuede at each short end of the stitched-together ribbons, sandwiching the ribbons between the Ultrasuede pieces, so that Ultrasuede and ribbon edges are flush.

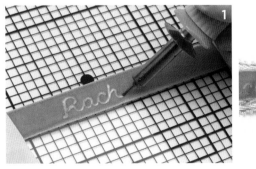

3. On one end, remove one of the top pieces of Ultrasuede and machine stitch a loop of cord to the edge to the remaining layers, through all layers. Make sure the loop is the right size to fit over the button before stitching it. Trim the ends of the cord and the loose threads.

4. Replace the Ultrasuede over the end with the loop, leaving the loop free, and sticking out of the fabric layers. Machine stitch the Ultrasuede pieces to each ribbon end, stitching close to the edge of the ribbon, through all layers of fabric. Trim off the excess Ultrasuede so that the edges are even with all ribbon edges. Be very careful not to clip off the closure loop when trimming.

5. Finish the edge of the suede with a blanket stitch (see page 55), using contrasting embroidery floss.

6. Using an embroidery needle and floss, sew button to the end without the loop, through all layers of fabric.

7. Stitch beads, shells, or other small embellishments to the finished cuff.

Caution

The heat-etching tool is extremely hot; do not touch any part of the metal while heated. Keep it on a heat-proof surface away from combustible materials. This tool is not appropriate for children and should only be used after reading manufacturer's instructions.

Felting

THE INTEREST IN FIBER ARTS has increased the popularity of felt and it is now widely available in an array of colors in yarn shops and online. Felt can be manipulated in a variety of ways, allowing a multitude of creative techniques to be explored. Bright colors combined with subtle hues produce exciting results. Wool has the advantage of being very soft and lightweight, which makes it ideal for jewelry design.

○ about felting ○

The process of felting wool involves "meshing" or interlocking the wool's fibers to make a dense, non-fraying material. If you view wool fiber through a microscope, you'll see that the surface is made up of scales. When the fibers are agitated (through washing or other abrasion) they catch on one another as they are rubbed together causing the fibers to permanently interlock, which results in a felted fabric.

There are two felting methods for felting small jewelry items or beads: wet felting and needle felting.

Wet Felting

Wet Felting is the process of combining agitation and hot and cold water to aid the felting process. Felt beads are made by rolling the wool to agitate the fibers. Hot water helps to open up the scales allowing the felting to begin. Pure soap, such as Ivory, also helps, acting as a lubricant that allows the fibers to move around more easily, thus speeding the process. (Detergents are less agitating to wool, so true soap is best.) Temperature differences between hot water and cold water "shock" the fibers, further agitating and shrinking them to compact into felt. When purchasing wool to make felted beads, look for 100% wool (roving or dyed felting fleece).

Needle Felting

Needle felting involves pushing a barbed needle through the wool fibers, which causes them to lock as the needle agitates the wool. This method is great for surface design as it allows you to felt layers of wool colors together. Wool felt or roving can be applied to another piece of felt by simply poking the barbed felting needle up and down through both layers until the fibers mesh and become attached.

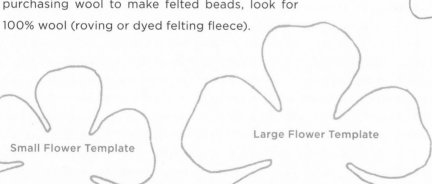

Leaf Template

Small Flower Template

Large Flower Template

Medium Flower Template

felt flower necklace

THE FLOWERS on this necklace are made using 100% wool felt sheets. After cutting the flower shapes from the felt, the wool is manipulated to further felt the fibers, thickening the felt and allowing you to sculpt the flower petals. Use the patterns provided to make these violet flowers, or make your own patterns to create a variety of different flower species.

MATERIALS & SUPPLIES

Wool felt sheets, one each in different colors of violet, one in olive green

Seed beads, small package

E or 6o, small package

Nylon thread, transparent or in color to match beads

Sharp beading needle

Bead thread, 24-inch length

Ribbon yarn, 2 yards

Bowl or sink filled with hot water

Small bowl filled with ice water

Liquid fabric stiffener and disposable container (optional)

Bar of pure soap such as Ivory

Towel

Fabric scissors

Fabric marking pencil

Wax paper

Fabric glue (optional)

1. Transfer the four templates on page 70, at 100%, to cardboard and cut them out. Lay the small, medium, and large flower templates onto the two shades of violet felt, and the leaf template onto the olive felt. Trace around templates onto the felt with a marking pencil and cut out a few of each size flower and a few leaves. Note: To make your own flower templates, separate the petals from an artificial flower and trace them onto paper or cardboard and cut out.

2. To further felt the felt flowers, soak them in hot water and then agitate the fibers using your fingers and a little bit of soap. Keep dipping them in the hot water, crunching and rubbing the petals between your fingers, as shown. The shapes will shrink in size as the fibers felt. When the flower pieces are at the desired size, rinse them in ice-cold water to remove any traces of soap and set the design. Pat the shapes dry with a towel.

3. If you prefer the look of soft flowers with less sculpted petals, you can skip this step. While the shapes are still damp, coat them with a diluted solution of fabric stiffener. This will give the felt added dimension by making it more rigid. Mix (very little) stiffener with water. Press the wool between your fingers to remove the excess.

4. While still damp, shape the petals with your fingers, as you would form clay. Pinch the tips to "cup" them and give them a natural appearance. Shape the leaves into cup shapes. Set them all on a piece of wax paper to dry.

5. After the petals dry, assemble them by stacking various size and/or color combinations. Stack two or three high, ending with smaller shapes on top.

6. To add beaded centers to the flowers, thread a beading needle with transparent nylon thread. Bring the needle up through the center of the petals (work through just one or two petal layers if three layers are difficult to sew through). Thread a few seed beads and then one larger "E" or 6o bead. Bring the needle back through the seed beads only (as shown) and then through to the underside of the petals. Repeat until the beaded center is as full as you would like, then knot the thread on the underside. Sew a few "E" or 6o beads to the olive leaf pieces. Sew stacked flowers from Step 5 together through all layers. To finish, knot and clip the thread on the bottom of the stack. Tip: You can glue the flowers together instead.

7. To make the twisted cord, cut one 2-yard length of ribbon yarn. Fold it in half and make a 1-inch loop. Tie a knot under the loop and secure the loop in a clipboard or by pinning or taping it to a table top. Twist the two ribbon strands together clockwise down the entire length. Using a beading needle and nylon bead thread, thread seed beads to create a 24-inch length of beads; tie it just under the ribbon loop, using an overhand knot (see page 108). Twist the twisted ribbon and the seed beads together counterclockwise; knot the ends securely. At the ends, leave a 9-inch (or more) tail of ribbon yarn to tie in a bow through the loop for the closure. Arrange the flowers along the twisted cord as desired, and stitch them to the cord with clear nylon thread.

felted bead bracelet

MAKING wet-felted beads is easier than it looks and it's also quite fun. This is a perfect project to make with kids. The beads felt up quickly, so you can make a bunch of colorful beads in a single afternoon. Add beads and sequins to the finished felt beads for sparkle.

MATERIALS & SUPPLIES

Dyed wool felt roving or fleece, one small bundle will make all the beads you need for this project

Sequins and seed beads

Handsewing needle

Quilting thread

Large, pointed needle to string beads with eye large enough to accommodate elastic

Elastic cord, 12 inches of heavy-duty, or 24 inches of lightweight cord (double lightweight cord when stringing)

Super Glue (Cyanoacrylate glue)

Small jump ring

Eyepin

Beads (optional), any beads that will accomodate elastic cord

Bowl or sink filled with hot water

Small bowl filled with ice water

Bar of pure soap such as Ivory

Towel

1. Pull out a strand of wool roving or fleece, separating it loosely with your fingers to fluff it up a bit.

2. Begin loosely winding the wool strand into a ball. Work as though you were winding a ball of yarn. Add more wool as needed to increase the size of the ball; shift the direction of the winding in order to keep the ball consistently round.

3. Keep winding until the ball is about the size of a walnut. The finished beads will end up being about half the size of the original ball of wool, so adjust the size of the initial ball of wool to accommodate the desired finished size.

4. Dip the wool ball in hot water (as hot you are comfortable touching). Squeeze out a bit of the water.

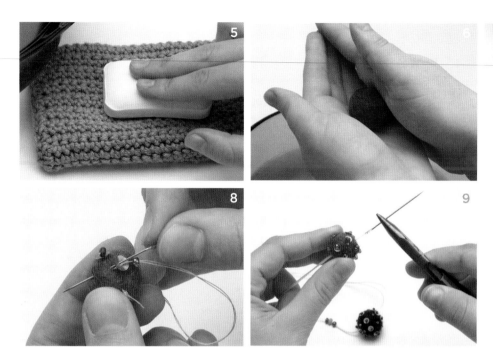

5. Lubricate your hands with a little bar soap.

6. Begin rolling the ball, softly, in the palms of your hands, like dough. Don't apply too much pressure or the ball will fold over on itself making a permanent fold or crease. As you practice you will develop a "feel" for the wool and be able to catch a fold in time to fix it. (See *Fixing a Folded Ball,* left.)

7. Continue dipping the ball in hot water as you roll, rinsing the soap out as you work. As the fibers condense and compact the ball will become smaller. At this stage you can gradually apply more pressure as you roll, until the ball feels very firm. For a tight ball, apply a lot of pressure with your palms at the end of the process. Rinse out soap residue with hot water. To shock the fibers and set the wool, dip or rinse the balls in ice-cold water. Blot the beads with a towel and let them dry.

8. Use a needle with quilting thread to sew seed beads and sequins onto the felt beads. Hide the thread knot under a sequin, anchoring it in the wool. Bring the needle up through the sequin, through the bead, and back down through the sequin. Sew through the felt ball and bring the needle up to sew on the next sequin. Continue to cover the ball and finish by knotting the thread under a sequin. Add a dot of fabric glue for extra security.

9. To string the beads, use a needle with an eye large enough for the elastic that will also fit through the bead. If you are using lightweight elastic, double it (knotting it at the ends). Pliers may make it easier to pull the needle and elastic through the bead. String felt, wood, and glass beads, alternating them to complete the design. To finish the elastic ends, tie a square knot (see page 111) and add a drop of glue to prevent fraying. Optional: To create a dangle, add beads to an eye pin, forming a loop at the top of the head pin. Attach loop to a jump ring, and hang over the elastic between the beads.

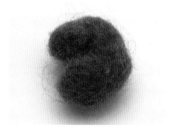

Fixing a Folded Ball

If your bead forms a fold, pull the fibers apart with your fingers and reshape the ball as you continue rolling. If you have a bead that won't unfold, it can be used as the core to form a larger bead—simply wrap more wool around the folded piece. Or, use your rejects to make funny felt creatures—the creases make good mouths.

needle-felted heart pendant

THESE beads employ a combination of techniques—wet felting to make the heart bead shape, and then needle felting to embellish the surface. Felted shapes take a bit of practice, so you might want to practice making a few round felted beads before making the hearts.

MATERIALS & SUPPLIES

Dyed wool fleece or roving, red, small ball

Felting needle

Fine handsewing needle to sew on beads

All-purpose thread

Large needle (long enough to pierce the length of the felt bead)

Quilting or button thread

Seed beads to decorate finished felt bead

Cord to form necklace: 2 yards variegated fiber, cut into two 1-yard pieces, any novelty fibers will work

#18 nylon cord, 1 yard

Glass beads to decorate the variegated cord and to add to the base of the felt bead

Button for closure, any type or size to suit design

Thread Zap tool or lighter to melt cord

Bowl or sink filled with hot water

Small bowl filled with ice water

Bar of pure soap such as Ivory

Fabric glue or seam sealant

Towel

1. Make a felt bead, following Steps 1 to 6 on pages 75–76. Take the beads, wring out some of the water, and begin to compress and mold the ball into a heart shape. Start by forming a triangle with a defined point at the bottom. Make an indentation with your fingers at the top to form the top of the heart, as shown. Push, pull, and compress the heart as though the wool were clay, continuing to dip the wool into hot water as you work it. As the heart starts to take shape, increase the pressure to further reduce the size and tighten the fibers. Rinse the heart in ice-cold water to set it and remove all traces of soap. Let dry.

2. To needlefelt the design, pull of a long strand of roving from the wool and roll and twist it into a tight strand. Attach an end of the strand to the heart bead with the felting needle by poking the needle repeatedly, straight up and down (vertically) into the felt, causing the fibers of the strand to "meld or bond" to the felted heart bead. Coil the strand along the bead to create a design, continuing to needle felt all along the strand.

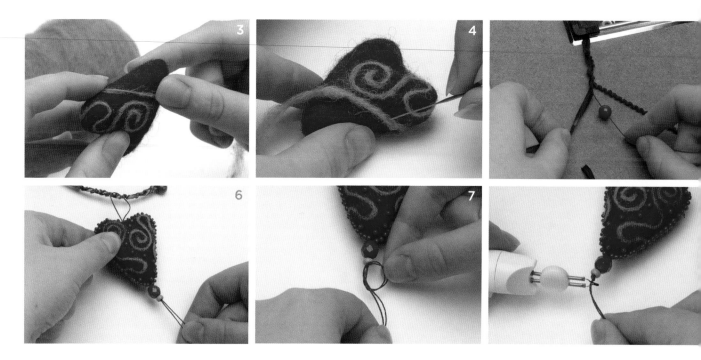

3. Change colors by pulling off a new strand of wool and twisting it to the end of the previously felted strand.

4. Continue to needlefelt new strands to cover the bead, as shown. Using a fine handsewing needle and all-purpose thread, stitch seed beads onto and around the edge of the felted heart bead with strong thread to further embellish the bead.

5. To make the braided cord and looped closure, cut 1 yard each of two decorative fibers and 1 yard of nylon cord. Tie all three cords into a knotted loop to create a closure that fits over the button. Secure the looped end in a clipboard. Braid the two fibers and the nylon cord, adding glass beads to the cord along the way, as shown. Weave the ends of the loop into the braid.

6. To add the felted heart bead to the braided cord, thread a long needle with nylon cord, and push the needle and cord vertically up through the center of the heart. Loop the cord over the finished braid and then push the needle and cord back through the center of the heart. Pull both ends to tighten the bead on the braid, as shown. Add a few decorative beads to the cord at the bottom of the heart.

7. To secure the beads, tie an overhand knot (see page 108) with the ends of the cord.

8. Melt the ends of the cord with a wax-melting tool (or lighter), which finishes them off so they won't fray. To finish the necklace, thread a shank button onto the end of the braided cord that does not have a loop and secure it with knots. Seal the ends of the cords with fabric glue or hem sealant.

Crochet
and Hook

CROCHET IS A VERSATILE craft for jewelry making. You can make a simple chain of crochet stitches to form a cord, or create rows of crochet stitches to build a form or base for a project. Because crochet stitches can be formed in the round, they are perfect for making flowers and circle motifs.

crochet stitches

HERE are the all the basic crochet stitches you'll need to know to make the crocheted and hooked jewelry designs that follow. Even if you've never crocheted or hooked before, a little practice will allow you to complete any of these designs.

There are a few terms to note before you start practicing the stitches:

- **Yarn Over:** Though it's not a stitch, yarn over is a term you will see throughout the instructions. To make a yarn over, simply bring the hook under the yarn so that the yarn is wrapped over the hook.

- **✳:** When you see a * in the instructions, it indicates a sequence of stitches to be repeated. This repeated sequence begins with a * followed by a second *, which indicates the end of the sequence.

- **Slip Knot:** A slip knot is often used when you attach the yarn to the hook before you begin stitching. Illustrated instructions for making the slip knot are on page 87, Steps 1 to 4.

- **Turn:** In crochet patterns, "turn" means you will be starting a new row. At the end of a row, the extra chain stitch that you make is called the "turning stitch." Right after you make this stitch you flip or "turn" the work over so that you can begin the new row, by working your way back down the previous row, starting at the turning stitch and ending at the beginning of the previous row.

CHAIN STITCH

Place a slipknot on your crochet hook. Yarn over hook and pull it through the slipknot to form a new loop on the hook. This is the first chain stitch. Repeat to form as many chain stitches as indicated in the project instructions. Note: In patterns, the first slip knot on the hook is not included when counting the number of chain stitches.

JOINING A RING

A slip stitch can be used to form a ring of stitches. To make a ring, first make a foundation chain as specified in the pattern instructions, and then work a slip stitch into the first chain to create, or join, the ring, as shown.

SLIP STITCH

Insert the hook into the indicated stitch, yarn over hook, and draw the loop through both the stitch and the loop on the hook. The slip stitch is often used to finish off the work—when you make the last stitch, pull the yarn tight and weave the end of the yarn into to hide it.

SINGLE CROCHET

Insert the crochet hook into the indicated stitch, yarn over hook, and pull the yarn through the stitch to form a loop on the hook; there are now two loops are on your hook. Yarn over hook and draw loop through both loops on hook, as shown.

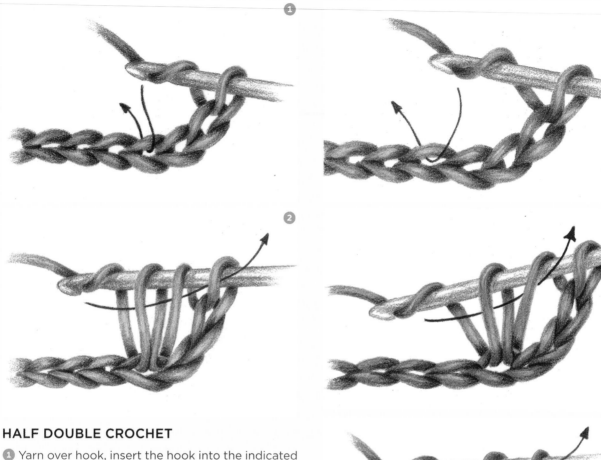

HALF DOUBLE CROCHET

① Yarn over hook, insert the hook into the indicated stitch, yarn over hook and pull the loop through the stitch; there are now three loops on hook.

② Yarn over hook and draw loop through all three loops on hook.

DOUBLE CROCHET

① Yarn over hook, insert hook into indicated stitch, yarn over hook and pull loop through the stitch; there are now three loops on hook.

② Yarn over hook and draw loop through two loops on hook.

③ Yarn over hook and draw loop through remaining two loops on hook.

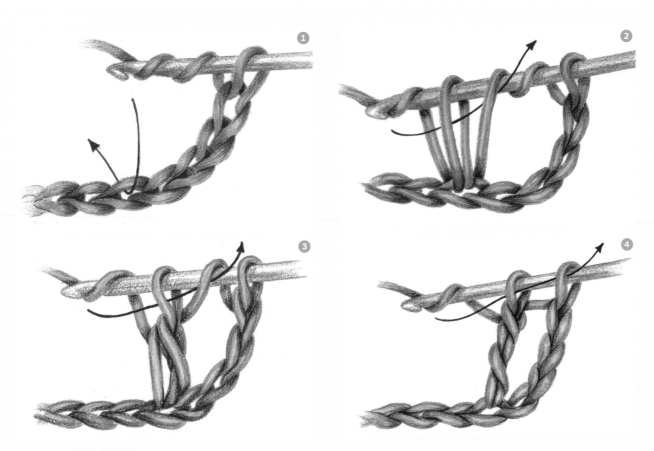

TRIPLE CROCHET

1 (Yarn over hook) twice, insert hook into indicated stitch, yarn over hook and pull up a loop through the stitch; there are now four loops on hook.

2 Yarn over hook and draw loop through two loops on hook; there are now three loops on hook.

3 Yarn over hook and draw loop through two loops on hook; there are now two loops on hook.

4 Yarn over hook and draw loop through remaining two loops on hook.

BEAD CHAIN

Move a bead up next to the hook, yarn over hook and draw loop through the loop on the hook, locking bead into the stitch, as shown.

crocheted fabric bracelet

RIBBON yarn made with fabric fiber is sturdy enough to hold a nice shape for a simple cuff style bracelet. The bracelet is very quick and easy to make. Vintage Bakelite buttons were used to create decorative closures that coordinate with the colors in the ribbon yarn. You could make your own buttons out of polymer if you don't have matching ones handy. These bracelets were finished with one row of single crochet stitches, but you can add rows for a wider cuff. Add beads and dangles, if you wish, attaching them with yarn.

Materials & Supplies

Mirah's Crafts Batik Ribbon Yarn), colors: Marigold, Buttercup, Crush, Lollipop, one ball or skein for each bracelet, or bias cut fabric strips

Crochet hook size I/9 (5.5 mm) or larger depending on the weight of the ribbon yarn

Large button for closure

Handsewing needle

All-purpose thread

1. Steps 1 to 4 show how to make a slip knot. First, make a loop near the end of the yarn, as shown.
2. Bring the working yarn (yarn from the ball/skein) up through the loop, making a second loop through the first.
3. Insert the hook into the loop created in Step 2.
4. Tighten the first loop by pulling on the working yarn and the tail, as shown, to complete the slip knot. You will now have one loop on your hook.

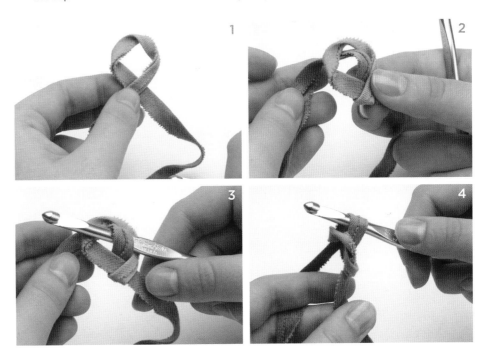

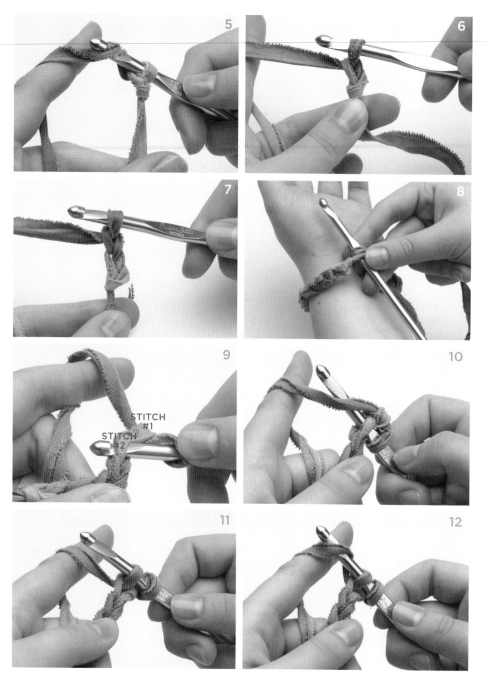

5. Wrap the yarn over the hook and pull the yarn through the loop on the hook. Count this as your first chain stitch.

6. This is what the finished chain stitch should look like.

7. To make more chain stitches, repeat Steps 5 and 6, counting each stitch as you go.

8. Crochet a row of chain stitches until the chain fits loosely around your wrist.

9. Begin a row of single crochet stitches by slipping the hook into the second stitch from the hook. The photo shows the hook in the stitch.

10. Hook the yarn over and pull the yarn through this chain stitch.

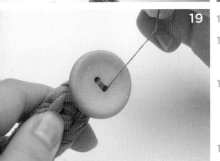

11. Now you have two loops on the hook.

12. Hook the yarn over again, this time you will be pulling the yarn through both loops on the hook completing the stitch.

13. This photo shows the completed first single crochet stitch. Count this as stitch number one of your first row. Continue making single crochet stitches along the chain until you reach the end of the row.

14. At the end of the first row, crochet one chain stitch. This photo shows the yarn over the hook to begin the chain stitch at the end of the row. The chain stitch is completed in Step 15.

15. Pull the yarn through the loop to complete the chain stitch. This photo shows the completed chain at the end of the row.

16. Continue on with a series of chain stitches that will form the loop closure. Measure the chain stitches to check the fit over the button to be used for the closure.

17. Insert the hook into the first stitch at the beginning of the chain, yarn over and pull the yarn through both loops on the hook, leaving one loop on the hook.

18. Cut off the yarn leaving a tail of about 6 inches. Pull the tail of the yarn through the loop with a slip stitch to finish. Pull the tail end of the yarn tight. Weave the end of the yarn through a few stitches to hide, cut off the excess.

19. Sew a button to the other end with a needle and thread. Knot the thread on the backside of the work.

crocheted choker

Project by **Michelle Ross**

BLACK is a classic, timeless color—it can be fancy or casual depending on what you wear with it. This choker is a fast project to make, so it's the perfect choice if you need to make a quick evening accessory. The fiber used can be found in specialty yarn stores, or you can substitute a similar weight fiber, if desired.

MATERIALS & SUPPLIES

Louisa Harding "Glisten" or similar ribbon yarn, one ball

Crochet hook, size 4 mm (G/6)

Tape measure or ruler

Stitch marker

Stainless steel T-pins for blocking

Foam core or other surface to block on

Iron or steamer

Shank button for closure, any size that works with design

Nine faceted drop or round glass beads (use a larger bead for the center focal point)

Nine head pins

Round-nose pliers

Wire cutters

1. Chain loosely for 16 inches—the length of the choker. Single crochet in each Chain to create a crochet strip.
2. Fold the crochet strip in half and place the stitch marker at the center.
3. Chain 1 at the end of the row and turn, single crochet 1 stitch in each of the first 2 stitches along the row. Chain 5, as shown.
4. Single Crochet over the strip (the yarn is crocheted over the entire strip with a single crochet stitch; make the stitch snug for a scalloped edge).

5. *Chain 5, Single Crochet over the strip at the end of the Chain 5 length* repeat from * to *. Repeat this pattern until you approach the center marker. You should have seven completed scalloped loops.

6. At the end of the seventh scalloped loop, crochet 2 single crochet over, chain 6, 2 single crochet over before starting the scalloped pattern again, as shown. Chain 5, single crochet over, repeat the same pattern as in Step 5 until you have an equal number of loops as the other side (seven loops on each side with one loop in the center). Single crochet in the last 2 stitches on the row as you did in Step 3 when you began the row.

7. Crochet enough chain stitches to make a loop for the closure. Measure the length to fit over the button when formed into a loop. Insert the hook into the first stitch on the choker to complete loop. Make 1 slip stitch to finish. Cut thread and pull through the last stitch. Weave in ends to hide.

8. Block the necklace by pinning it to the foam core, accentuating the scallops and loops. Steam or dampen with water to set the shape of the choker. Allow to dry (you can speed things up by using a a hair dryer if you wish). Sew a button to the end opposite the loop using the tail end of the yarn.

9. Add beads to head pins and attach them to the scallops using round-nose pliers to form loops at the top. Wrap the loop at the base of the loop on top of the bead and clip off the excess wire.

crocheted flowers wristband

Project by **Michelle Ross**

CROCHET cotton is available in a rainbow of colors, giving you lots of options for your design. This bracelet can also be made in an evening version—add sparkle with glass bead or pearl embellishments to the flowers and/or cuff. For a variation, make small individual flowers to sew along a thin crocheted band, like the brown bracelet in the photo on page 99.

Instruction Note To maintain the pattern of crochet stitches for this bracelet, you must keep the stitches to a multiple of 5, plus 1 turning stitch (Multiple of 5 + 1). These directions are for a 6½-inch wrist. To begin, chain 41 stitches (8 x 5, plus 1 turning stitch = 41 stitches). Adjust the number of stitches up or down for your wrist measurement, keeping a multiple of 5 + 1 stitches.

⊰ wristband ⊱

Materials & Supplies

Pearl cotton #8, two balls

Crochet hook, size B/1 (2.25 mm)

Yarn or tapestry needle

Floss threaders

Seed beads (Delica type)

Various glass beads

Four snaps, any type and size that works with design

Handsewing needle

All-purpose thread

1. **With 2 strands held together. Chain 41 stitches. For the first row, single crochet in second chain from hook, complete 40 single crochet stitches to finish the row. Begin the second row by turning the work, chain 5.**

2. **Skip 2 single crochet stitches, 1 double crochet stitch in each of the next 3 single crochet stitches. Chain 2, skipping 2 single crochet stitches**

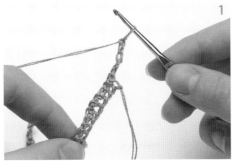 

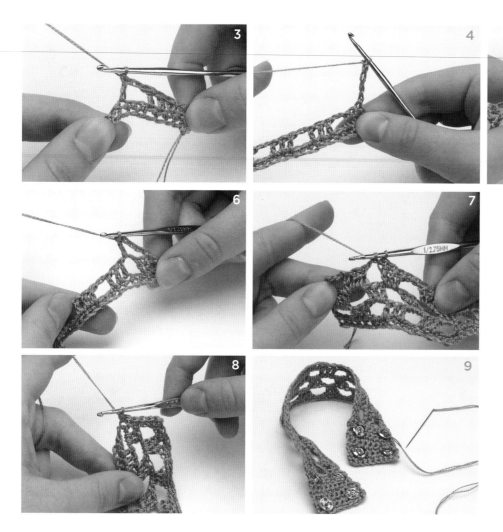

3. 1 double crochet in next 3 stitches as in Step 2. This photo shows one completed double crochet stitch. Repeat pattern across to the end of the row.

4. Row 3: Turn, chain 5

5. *3 double crochet over the 2 chain stitches (from the previous row) through the open space, chain 2*. Repeat from * to *. The row ends with 3 double crochet stitches.

6. This photo shows the first finished double crochet stitches from Step 5.

7. Row 4: Turn, chain 5, repeat pattern from last row across, the row ends with 3 double crochet stitches. Row 5: Chain 1, turn, single crochet in each stitch across to the end of row.

8. Turn down to crochet across the short side; Single crochet about 8 to 10 stitches, inserting the needle into the work along the side until you reach the end.

9. Chain 1 stitch at the end of row and turn to single crochet across another row. Continue rows of single crochet until you have about 1¹⁄₂ inch of rows at the end of cuff. Cut off thread and finish off with a slip stitch knot. Weave the ends back into the work to hide. With new thread single crochet rows on the other side in the same manner. Check the bracelet for fit, add rows as needed. Sew on four snaps.

⁂{ large flower }⁜

1. Use two strands of pearl cotton, string on 80 delica or seed beads (plus some extra) to the double strand using a bead needle or floss threader. Chain 6, join with a slip stitch to form a ring.
2. Chain 3
3. Work 15 double crochet in ring = 16 double crochet stitches. Note: The stitches are formed over the ring.
4. Join to top of third chain stitch with a slip stitch to complete the ring.
5. Chain 4
6. *Skip 1 double crochet stitch, insert the hook into the next stitch and join with a slip stitch* to create a scallop or loop, repeat around = eight chained scallops.

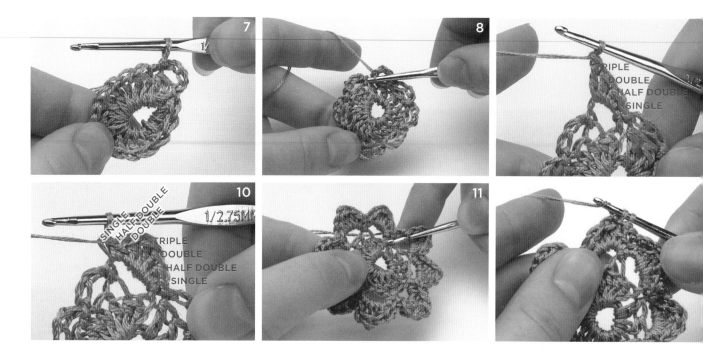

7. The completed scallop after joining.

8. Insert the hook next to the first scallop (next to the base) in the ring to finish the ring of scallops with a slip stitch.

9. In each scallop crochet the following sequence to form each petal around: *1 single crochet, 1 half double, 1 double crochet, 1 triple crochet, 1 double crochet, 1 half double, 1 single crochet* = 7 stitches total to form one petal. Repeat around. This photo shows half of the scallop.

10. This photo shows the whole scallop.

11. Insert the hook the hook between the petals with a slip stitch.

12. To crochet the beads around the edge of the flower, slide 1 bead up to work per stitch. With the working yarn in front slide a bead up, go into the back loop of each stitch from back to front, yarn over and pull through both loops with a slip stitch to hold the bead in place. Continue adding a bead to each stitch around the flower. (See page 85 for instructions for adding beads.) To finish, insert hook between the last petal in the loop at top of the double crochet ring and pull up snugly. Fasten off with a slip stitch and weave the tail towards the center to hide the end.

{ small flower }

(see photos for large flower)

1. Chain 5, join with a slip stitch to make a ring.
2. Chain 2, 10 single crochet stitches around the ring, join to top of chain 2.
3. Chain 3, skip 1 single crochet stitch, join with slip stitch in next single crochet stitch, repeat around = Five (chain 3) loops.
4. Make petals same as for large flower (see steps 8 to 11), fasten off, weave the tail in to hide.

{ attach the flowers to the cuff }

Use about ¾ yard single strand of pearl cotton, stack the small flower onto the larger one and stitch to the center of the cuff.

{ make the beaded center }

Sew on beads, stringing several in a row to give height to the "beaded stamens" in the center. With the thread coming up through the center, string 3 to 4 beads on the thread, skip the last bead (to hold the thread) and stitch down through the rest through to the back of the cuff. Continue stitching on beads until the center is as full as you want.

TRIPLE CROCHET 2 TOGETHER

Yarn over twice, insert hook in next stitch (or loop), yarn over and draw through loop, yarn over and draw through two loops, yarn over and draw through two loops, (leave two loops on hook) yarn over twice, insert hook into the same loop (in this pattern), yarn over and draw through loop, yarn over and draw through two loops, yarn over and draw through two loops, (three loops on hook) yarn over and draw through all three loops.

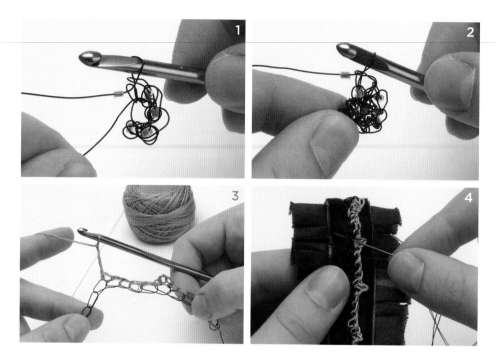

❈{ small wire flower }❈

This flower is similar to the large flower, but with fewer rows, and it has eight petals instead of ten.

1. (Photograph shows the center of the flower.) To begin flower, 2 chain stitches, Single crochet 8 stitches into the first chain. Slip stitch into the first single crochet stitch to join the round (or ring). Chain 6 *Double crochet into next Single crochet stitch of first row, chain 3*. Repeat around from * to * until there are eight loops, slip stitch into the third chain of the first loop to complete the round. For the center, thread about twenty beads onto wire. You will be adding one bead with each stitch. Row 1: Chain 2, 4 single crochet into the first chain stitch (add a bead with each stitch).

2. Row 2: 2 single crochet stitches into each single crochet stitch of the previous row (add a bead with each stitch). Thread a large-eyed needle with wire and sew large flower, small flower, and center together, hiding the ends of the wire inside.

3. Crochet a chain of wire to match the length of the finished bracelet from snap to snap. Clip off the wire. Crochet along the wire with pearl cotton with a single crochet stitch. Make a picot every fifth stitch. (A picot is made by chaining 3, single crochet into the same chain stitch.) Single Crochet in next 5 chains. Repeat *single crochet 5, one picot, single crochet 5* to the end of the chain.

4. Stitch the crocheted wire down the center of the bracelet on top of the velvet ribbon. Sew the flower to the center with needle and thread.

⁕{ crocheted wire necklace }⁕

MATERIALS & SUPPLIES

Dritz snap, size 1 for the closure

28 gauge craft wire, black, 1 spool

Crochet hook, size B/1 (2.75mm)

DMC Pearl Cotton, size 12, 1 ball

Seed beads

Sewing needle

1. Make the large flower as directed for the bracelet (Steps 1 to 11 for wire flower).

2. Make the center as directed in Step 2 for the center of small flower above, except this center has more rows:

   To begin Row 1: slide 60 beads onto the wire, chain 2 stitches, single crochet 4 stitches in 1st chain stitch adding a bead with each stitch. Slip stitch together to join the ring (round). Row 2: 2 single crochet stitches in each single crochet stitches from the previous rows, adding a bead with each stitch. Row 3: 2 single crochet stitches in each single crochet stitches from the previous rows, adding a bead with each stitch. Sew the beaded center to the larger flower with wire.

3. For the neck wire, hook a series of chain stitches along the wire to the desired length. The necklace in the photo on page 100 is 17 inches long. Make two identical chains.

4. With pearl cotton single crochet stitch into each of the chain stitches along the wire. Make a picot every nine stitches (picot = chain 3, single crochet into the same loop of the wire chain stitch). Repeat along the length of the chain; repeat on the other wire chain.

5. To finish the ends, hold the ends of two chain strands together, tie wire to one strand. Chain 1, single crochet into each strand. Repeat twice to make three rows. Complete the connection at the other end of the necklace to connect the ends.

6. Sew a snap at the ends with wire and a needle. Sew the large flower to the center of the strands to finish the necklace.

Knotting and Braiding

FIBERS THAT ARE KNOTTED or woven together provide both strength and a foundation for other elements in jewelry designs. Braids borrowed from ancient techniques and simple knots used in macramé offer ample options for creating a variety of intricate patterns for your jewelry designs.

knots

THE KNOTS favored by sailors and Boy Scouts are the same as those used in jewelry making, and they can be both decorative and functional. Macramé, the art of tying a sequence of traditional knots to create a design pattern, is easy to master. Practice these simple knots to complete any of the jewelry projects that follow.

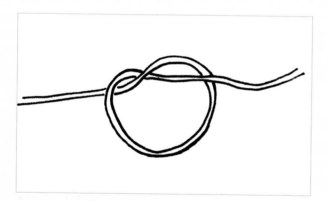

OVERHAND KNOT

This is a very simple knot. To tie it, make a loop with the cord, bring one end of the cord through the loop, and pull tight.

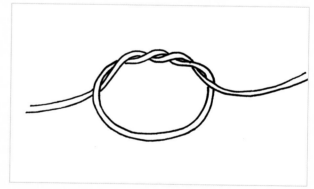

BARREL KNOT

This knot is similar to the overhand knot. The trick is to keep the tension nice and even so that one wrap isn't tighter than the others, causing the knot to bunch up.

Make a loop, then bring one end of the cord through the loop and wrap it around the cord three to five times. Pull the cord to tighten the knot.

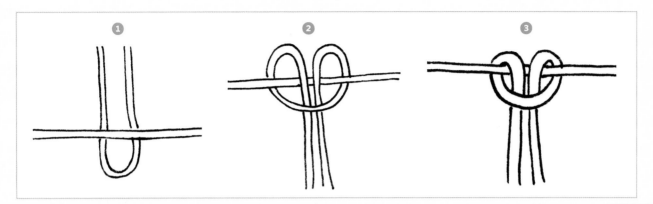

LARK'S HEAD KNOT

This knot is used to attach or mount a cord to a foundation cord, ring (see plastic ring on page 113), or other support.

1 Fold a cord in half to create a loop, then bring the loop *under* the foundation cord.

2 Bring the ends of the cord through the loop.

3 Pull the ends snugly over the foundation cord to finish.

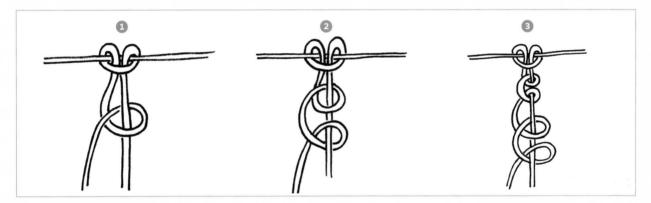

LARK'S HEAD SENNET

This is a row of lark's head knots tied over one or more foundation cords to form a chain, or sennet (a sequence of knots). This is the same knot pattern used in tatting, a traditional lacemaking technique.

If you see a break in the pattern, it's probably because you accidentally tied the same loop twice. In that case, pull out the knots to correct the mistake by following the over-under pattern along the chain. Practice a few knots after looking at the illustrations.

1 Tie a lark's head knot to a foundation cord. Bring one of the cords extending from the knot (this becomes the working cord) up and over the foundation cord; next, loop it under the foundation cord and out through the loop as shown. This forms the first half of the knot. Pull this loop snug against the foundation cord.

2 To tie the second half of the knot, bring the working cord under the foundation cord this time, looping it over the cord and through.

3 To create the chain, you always tie the first half of the knot over the foundation cord and the second half of the knot under the foundation cord.

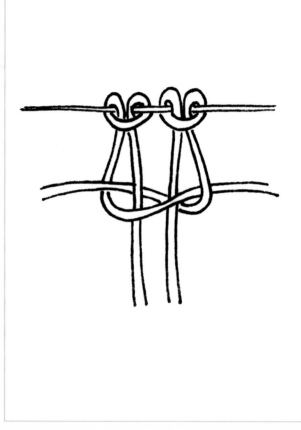

ALTERNATING HALF HITCH

Tie one cord (the working cord) over a foundation cord, then switch so that the working cord now becomes the foundation cord. Tie the working cord (previously the foundation cord) over the new foundation cord. Continue switching back and forth, tying one around the other to form the pattern. Keep the tension even for each knot.

HALF KNOT

A half-knot is the first half of a square knot, although it can be tied alone. If you tie a chain of half-knots, you'll get a spiral or twist. The example shown here begins with four cords mounted to a foundation cord.

To tie a half-knot, bring the left cord over the two middle (foundation) cords, like an "L" shape. Bring the right cord over the tail of the left cord, then under the two middle (foundation) cords and up through the left loop as shown. Pull the knot tightly against the middle (foundation) cords to secure.

SQUARE KNOT (FLAT KNOT)

The square knot consists of two opposite half knots. It is probably the most popular knot used in macramé. Tie a half knot, then tie a second, mirror image half knot directly under it. (The first half knot starts with the cord on the left side, the second half knot starts with the cord on the right side.) After tying the first half knot, bring the right cord over the two center cords. Bring the left cord over the tail of the right cord and under the center cords, then back up through the loop on the right; pull taut. Practice this knot with two colors of cord to help you visualize the over-and-under path.

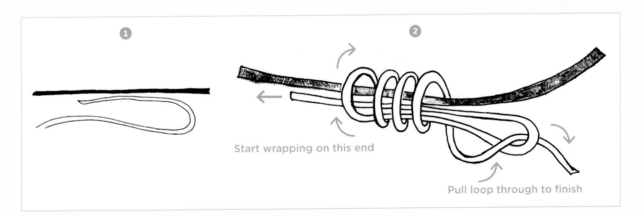

Start wrapping on this end

Pull loop through to finish

WRAPPED FINISHING KNOT

This knot is used to neatly wrap a single cord or bundle of cords. It makes a decorative finish for the end of a cord, or it can be used as a slide closure for a necklace or bracelet.

1. To form the knot, fold the wrapping (working) cord to make a loop as shown. Hold this folded cord (loop) next to the foundation cord that you will be wrapping.

2. Start wrapping the working cord over itself and the foundation cord, wrapping toward the fold (loop). When you are satisfied with the number of wraps, bring the end of the working cord through the loop. Pull both ends of the cord tightly to finish. Clip off the ends of the cord and seal them to prevent fraying.

tatted ring bracelet

TATTING is a form of lacemaking, which is essentially a series of lark's head knots tied in a row or (sennet). A tatting shuttle is not required for this project because each length of cord is fairly short to cover each ring. A magnetic clasp provides a nice "hidden" closure for this funky 60s style bracelet.

Materials & Supplies

Metallic yarn, any type, 2 yards per ring

Wrights Boye® Cabone Rings, five size 1½ inch, or similar plastic rings

Magnetic clasp, any type or size

Crochet hook, any size

Handsewing needle

Quilting or button thread

Fabric glue, any type

1. The yarn-covered rings on this bracelet consist of a series of lark's head knots, or sennets. You'll need about 2 yards of yarn per ring. Attach yarn to a ring with a lark's head knot (see page 109), leaving an 8-inch tail.

2. Starting with the long end (the working yarn), make a lark's head sennet knot (see page 109).

3. Continue around the ring with the under, over sennet pattern until the ring is covered. This photo shows the progression of the knots; notice the yarn is OVER the ring.

4. Make five rings (or the number that fits your wrist). When rings are covered, leave at least a 6-inch tail of yarn on each ring. Connect the covered rings by threading the tails from one ring through the knots of another with a small crochet hook.

5. Tie the ends of the cord with a square knot to secure. Clip off the ends and seal with fabric glue.

6. Using a needle and quilting or button thread, stitch a magnetic clasp to each end of the bracelet.

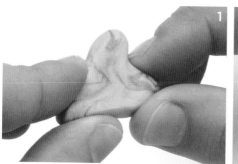

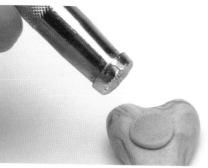

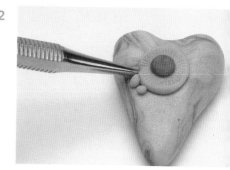

braided cord necklace with polymer clay pendant

KUMIHIMO, is a well known Japanese braid making technique in which cords or fibers are intertwined with the use of a round stand and little spools of cord. Similar braid-making techniques can be found from other cultures as well, with variations in the stand employed and in the number of cords used to create different braid patterns. This project uses a clever cord maker that is reminiscent of the Kumihimo stand, used to make a round braid with colorful fibers.

MATERIALS & SUPPLIES

Diva Custom Cord Maker kit (Fiber Goddess)

Binder clip (included in kit, above)

Yarn bobbins, seven (included in kit, above)

Lengths of various fibers or cords; seven in total, each cut to 1 yard in length, any cord or fiber can be used, just make sure they are generally the same weight

Hypo Cement or white fabric glue

Sculpey or Premo polymer clay (Polyform Products), small amounts

Leather stamping tool for texture

Plastic coated wire Fun Wire™ (Toner Plastics) or other plastic coated wire that can be baked with the polymer clay, small piece

Glass rhinestone

End caps for cord, two

24-gauge silver wire, 12 inches in length

Clasp finding (lobster claw and ring)

Round-nose pliers

❧ polymer clay heart charms ☙

1. Condition (roll and squeeze) a small ball of polymer clay, swirling various colors if desired. (It's nice to use colors that coordinate with the colors you will be using for the braided cord.) Shape the clay into a heart with your fingers.

2. Decorate the clay heart with more colored clay; make a texture on the clay with a leather stamping tool.

3. Add decorative elements and details with small bits of clay.

4. Use the end of a tool or pencil eraser to push a glass rhinestone deeply into the center of the clay.

5. Form the Fun Wire into a loop large enough for your braided cord to fit through, twisting a coil around the base to secure the loop. Push the twisted base of the loop into the clay heart, as shown. Pack the clay around the wire to make sure it is buried and will not pull out after baking. Place the heart on a glass tile or baking dish and bake it, in a toaster oven dedicated for polymer clay, at 275° F for 30 minutes. Let the piece cool slowly in the oven to prevent cracking or splitting.

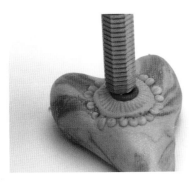
4

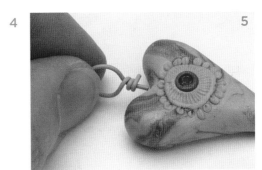
5

braided cord

1. Cut seven different colored cords (or fibers), each about 1 yard long, to wind on bobbins. (One length will yield a 16- to 18-inch necklace. For a longer necklace, cut the cord or fibers two to two-and-a-half times the desired finished length.) Open seven bobbins like a spool and wind a cord around each, leaving a 6-inch tail exposed. Close each spool to keep the cord from unwinding.

2. Gather the ends of all the cords and tie them all into an overhand knot (see page 108) to secure. Thread the knot through the center hole of the cord maker (use the cord maker with the hole that is the best fit for the cord to pass through). Attach a binder clip to the knotted end to weight the end of the cord as you work.

3. Flip the cord maker over so that the knot is hanging from the bottom, with the knot flush with the bottom of the cord maker. Pull each cord into a slot, leaving one empty. The bobbins will hang around the edge. Turn the cord maker so that the empty slot is closest to you (in the position of 6 o'clock), as shown. Before beginning, determine your working direction. If you are right-handed you will work in a clockwise direction (to the right); if you are left-handed you will work in a counter-clockwise direction (to the left). Starting at 6 o'clock, pick up the third cord from the empty slot. This photo shows the third (pink) cord on the right side (right-handed orientation).

4. Lift the cord over to the empty slot, as shown. (If you are left-handed, pick up the third cord to the left side of the empty slot.) Turn the cord maker clockwise

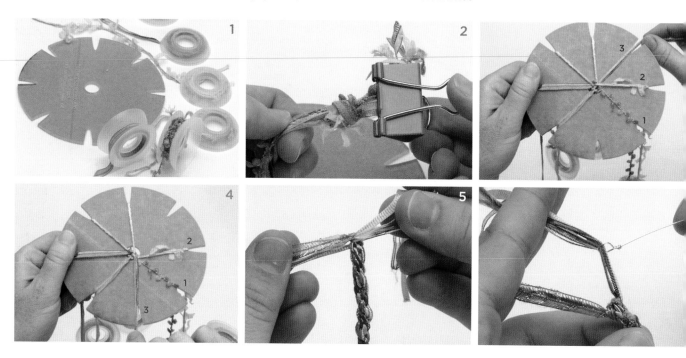

 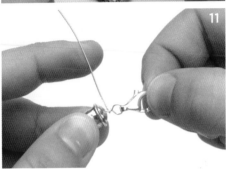

(counter clockwise for left-handers) to rotate the new empty slot to the 6 o'clock position. Repeat the process to braid the length of cord. Always work from the third cord on the same side, rotating the cord maker in the same direction, or the cord will unwind. Pull more cord from the bobbins as needed. Fiber Goddess suggests repeating: "Empty to Me, 1-2-3" to remember the braiding sequence.

5. As you pull more cords from the bobbins, hold the center of the cords with your thumb to keep them in place as you adjust the tension and length of the cords, as shown. Don't let bobbins hang too long or they will tangle. Move the binder clip up as needed to keep the cord weighted as you work. When the cord is the desired length, remove it from the cord maker and unwind the excess cord from bobbins. Split the cords into two sections (three cords in one hand and four in the other).

6. Cut a 6-inch piece of silver wire and form a twisted loop on the end and thread it over one group of cords on one side.

7. Tie a square knot (see page 111) with the sets of cords to secure the wire in place.

8. Clip off the ends of the cords close to the knot and apply glue to seal the fibers.

9. Slide the polymer heart charm onto the cord before adding the end caps. Slide the end caps over the wire, with the wire threaded through the hole of the end cap. Pull the ends of the cord tightly into the cap to conceal. A little more glue will help to anchor, if needed.

10. Use round-nose pliers to form a loop with the wire. Add a clasp and twist the end of the wire at the base. Clip off the excess wire.

11. Repeat the process to add the other end cap and ring clasp to finish the cord.

woven metal thread bracelets

VINTAGE metal thread is actually real metal applied to a thread core, not to be confused with "metallic" which is simply a synthetic material applied to the thread. Real metal thread has a weight associated with it; it actually feels a bit heavier and is stiffer than normal embroidery thread because of the metal content. Vintage types also tarnish to reveal a patina as they age. Add a vintage metal button for the perfect closure to match the finished bracelet.

Materials & Supplies

Metal thread, gold or silver, 8½ total yards

Weaving Wheel (Toner Plastics)

Vintage button with a shank

Binder clip

Fabric glue or seam sealant

Clipboard (or tape work to a secure surface such as a table or counter top)

Beads to sew along cord (optional)

Clear nylon thread (optional)

Handsewing needle (optional)

1. Cut four strands of metal thread: three strands 2 yards long, and one strand 2½ yards long. Hold all of the cords even at one end and measure to the mid-point of the shorter strands. At this point, use the longer strand to tie a series of lark's head sennets (see page 109), over the other three threads, which will be used to form a loop closure for the bracelet. Use a clipboard to hold the threads as you tie, as shown, or, tape or pin the threads to a fixed surface instead.

2. Continue tying knots until the sennet fits over your button when formed into a loop. Test the loop until it's big enough to fit over the button.

3. Hold the loop together and place it through the center of the wheel as shown. (The loop holds together at the base as the braid is formed. Or, if you prefer, you can tie a square knot (see page 111) at the base of the knot before placing it in the wheel). You will have eight working threads at the base of the wheel.

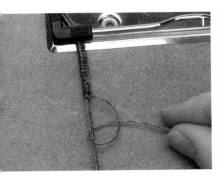

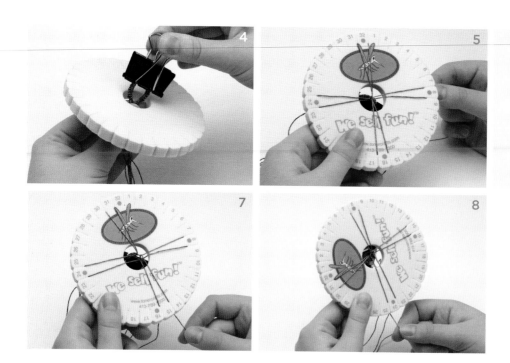

4. Clip a binder clip to the loop to hold it on the underside of the wheel.

5. Arrange the eight threads on the wheel as shown, pulling each through a slit to hold. Notice the numbers and the dots on the wheel to aid placement. Pull the threads to make the tension even, with all threads meeting in the center of the wheel, as shown.

6. To begin forming the braid, pull the thread between 16 and 17 on the wheel and bring the thread straight across to insert between 30 and 31, as shown. Another way to think of this step is: "bottom left thread to top left." This will help you remember where to move the thread as you work around the wheel.

7. Pull out the thread between 1 and 32 and bring the thread straight across to insert between 14 and 15. Or think of this step as "top right to bottom right."

8. Turn the wheel a quarter turn, in a counterclockwise direction, so that the next dot (#8) is at the top.

9. Repeat the steps for moving the thread as described in Steps 6 and 7: "bottom left to top left" and then "top right to bottom right." The photo shows that the thread that was between 24 and 25 has just been moved to the slit between 6 and 7 (bottom left to top left).

10. Now pull the thread from between 8 and 9 and move it to the slit between 22 and 23 (top right to bottom right), as shown. Turn the wheel a quarter turn in a counterclockwise direction to continue braiding. Continue moving the threads and turning the wheel to form the braid. Make sure to keep the tension even as you work. Occasionally measure the thread until it fits around your wrist.

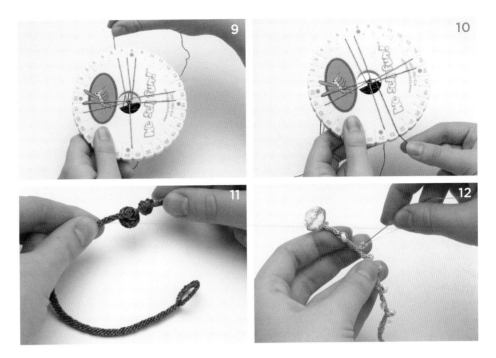

11. Remove the thread from the wheel and slide the shank of the button over the threads. Tie an overhand knot (see page 108) with all of the threads. Clip off the ends of the threads and seal with fabric glue that dries clear.

12. As a decorative option, sew beads along the thread with clear nylon thread. Hide the knotted ends of the thread inside the thread.

macramé bracelet

A FEW simple knots are used to tie a bracelet with a button and loop closure. Purchase beads with large holes to fit over the nylon cord. Macramé is a very portable craft; take this project on the go with you by using a clipboard to hold your work as you tie the knots.

MATERIALS & SUPPLIES

Nylon macramé cord (YLI Corp.), 7 yards total: cut one 3 yards long and two 2 yards long

round wooden beads, natural color

barrel shaped wooden beads, brown

Three silver cylinder shaped metal beads

Clipboard (or tape work to a secure surface such as a table or counter top)

Small piece of wire to thread beads

Button for closure

Thread Zap tool or lighter

1. Use a clipboard to hold the cords as you tie the macramé knots (or tape the cords to a table top). The longer cord will be tied around the other two. Find the mid-point along the two cords and tie a lark's head knot (see page 109) over the shorter cords with the longer one, as shown.

2. Tie a series of lark's head sennets (see page 109) over the two central cords with the longer cord, as shown. Keep tying the knots until the knotted cord is long enough to fit over your button when formed into a loop, then form a loop at the end of the knotted cord.

3. Place the formed loop into the clipboard to hold, as shown. Make sure to adjust all of the cords so they are even in length before continuing to knot. You can slide the finished lark's head knots along the central cords, if needed to adjust.

4. Tie a square knot over the four central (core) cords (see page 111). Tie a second square knot. The photo shows the finished knots.

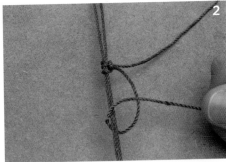

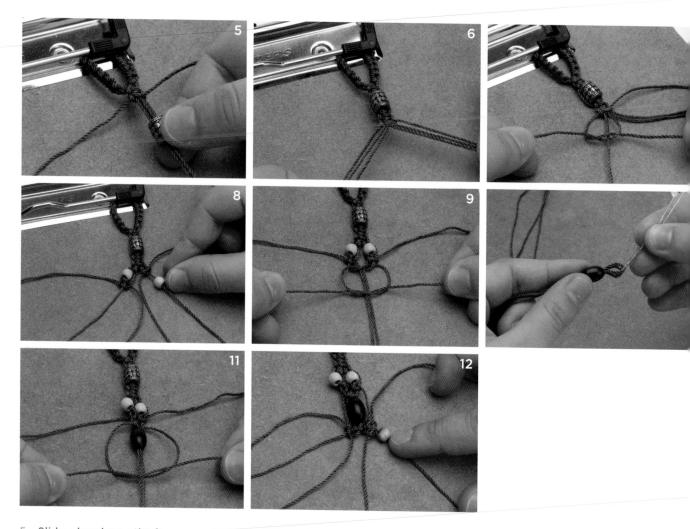

5. Slide a bead over the four core cords up close to the base of the square knots.

6. Tie two more square knots under the bead. Split the cords in half, holding three on each side, as shown.

7. With the three cords on the left, tie a square knot around one cord in the middle. Repeat on the right side with the other three cords.

8. Slide a bead up close to the knot on each side; tie a square knot beneath each bead.

9. Bring four cords to the middle and tie a square knot over the two center core cords, leaving the outside two cords free.

10. Thread a barrel shaped wooden bead over the central two cords. Use a bent wire to aid in threading the cord through the bead.

11. Tie a square knot under the bead with four cords (tie two over the center two, leaving the other two cords free). This photo shows the first half of the knot being tied.

12. Split the cords into two sections (three on each side). Tie a square knot with each set as you did in Step 7. Slide a bead up on each side under the knot, as in Step 8.

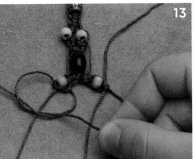

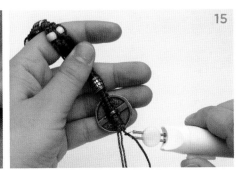

13. Tie a square knot under the beads on each side as you did in Step 8. This completes the macramé pattern, which is to be repeated for the rest of the bracelet.

14. Tie two square knots over the central four cords with two outside cords, as you did in Step 4. Follow Steps 4 to 13 to repeat the pattern until you have a length that fits your wrist, ending with a silver bead to match the one you started with. Add a few square knots as necessary until the bracelet fits properly.

15. Thread all six cords through the shank of a button. Tie an overhand knot (see page 108) with all of the cords. Use thread zap tool to fuse the fibers and finish the cord. A candle or lighter can also be used to melt the ends of the cord.

contributing artists

RACHEL HAAB (embroidered rings, quilted cuff bracelets)
www.stellardream.net

SHERRI HAAB
www.sherrihaab.com

MICHELLE ROSS (crocheted flower bracelets, crocheted black choker)
www.polymerclayplay.com

MARY STANLEY (hooked flower pins)
http://marystanley.blogspot.com

LISA TOLAND (wire crocheted bracelet, wire crocheted necklace)
www.lisatoland.com

suppliers

CLOVER
www.clover-usa.com
Felting needles, felt, yo-yo templates, crochet hooks

THE COLONIAL NEEDLE COMPANY
www.colonialneedle.com
Felting wools, felting needles, sewing notions and supplies

CRAFTER'S PICK
www.crafterspick.com
The Ultimate Glue, fabric and jewel glues

CREATIVE CASTLE
www.creativecastle.com
Seed beads, large hole beads, findings and supplies

DMC
www.dmc-usa.com
Embroidery floss, craft threads, crochet cottons, Senso, quilting thread

FIBER GODDESS
www.fibergoddess.net
Diva Custom Cord Maker

GS SUPPLIES
www.gssupplies.com
G-S Hypo Cement, G-S Fabric Cement

LACIS
www.lacis.com
Metal thread, tatting and crochet threads, embroidery supplies, ribbons, tools and supplies

MIRAH'S CRAFTS
www.balifab.com
Batik ribbon

NATIONAL NONWOVENS
www.woolfelt.com
WoolFelt, Wool Wisps (wool fleece)

PELLON
www.shoppellon.com
Fusible fleece, interlinings

POLYFORM PRODUCTS
www.sculpey.com
Premo and Sculpey polymer clay

PRYM CONSUMER
www.dritz.com
Covered button kits, eyelets and setters

STRANODESIGNS
http://stranodesigns.com
Velvet ribbon

THERM O WEB
www.thermoweb.com
HeatnBond Lite and HeatnBond Ultrahold iron-on adhesives

TINSEL TRADING COMPANY
www.tinseltrading.com
Metal threads, vintage flowers and leaves, trims, ribbons

TONER CRAFTS
www.tonercrafts.com
Weave Wheel, Fun Wire

ULTRASUEDE®
www.ultrasuede.com
Ultrasuede products, retailers listed on website

THE VINTAGE WORKSHOP
www.thevintageworkshop.com
Vintage images, printable fabric, CD collections

WALNUT HOLLOW
www.walnuthollow.com
Creative Textile Tool, tempered glass mat

WRIGHTS
www.wrights.com
Trims and ribbons, Boye cabone rings

YLI CORP.
www.ylicorp.com
Nylon macramé cord, threads, silk

Index

photo credits

All photographs by Dan and Sherri Haab, except those on
the following pages, which are by Zachary Williams.

Zachary Williams: 2, 9, 10, 12, 14, 16, 17, 18, 20, 21, 22, 24, 25,
26, 28, 30, 32 (Step 8), 34, 37, 38, 41, 42, 46-47, 48-49, 52,
57, 58, 60(Three at bottom), 62, 66, 68, 73, 74, 79, 80, 86,
90, 99, 100, 106, 112, 114, 119, 121, 122, 125